Specialty Breads *in* *Your* Bread Machine

Specialty Breads *in* *Your* Bread Machine

Norman A. Garrett

Sterling Publishing Co., Inc.
New York

Note: The nutrient values shown with the recipes in this book are approximations only and are shown strictly for comparison. Because nutrient values will vary according to the product brand, quantity, and type of ingredient used, individuals needing specific nutrient values should compute the values themselves. Neither the author nor the publisher represent these values to reflect the exact nutritional content of these recipes.

Results of these recipes will vary according to climatic conditions, proper use of ingredients, make and model of machine used, and freshness of ingredients. All recipes in this book have been thoroughly tested, but not on all available machines. The author and publisher make no guarantee as to the results of an individual recipe baked on a particular machine in a specific situation, since the possible combinations of variables are almost endless.

Library of Congress Cataloging-in-Publication Data

Garrett, Norman A.
    Specialty breads in your bread machine / Norman A. Garrett.
        p.   cm.
    Includes index.
    ISBN 0-8069-9511-4
    1. Bread.   2. Automatic bread machines.   I. Title.
    TX769.G73424   1998
    641.8'15—dc 21   98.40058
                                                             CIP

10   9   8   7   6   5   4   3   2   1

Published by Sterling Publishing Company, Inc.
387 Park Avenue South, New York, N.Y. 10016
©1998 by Norman A. Garrett
Distributed in Canada by Sterling Publishing
c/o Canadian Manda Group, One Atlantic Avenue, Suite 105
Toronto, Ontario, Canada M6K 3E7
Distributed in Great Britain and Europe by Cassell PLC
Wellington House, 125 Strand, London WC2R 0BB, England
Distributed in Australia by Capricorn Link (Australia) Pty Ltd.
P.O. Box 6651, Baulkham Hills, Business Centre, NSW 2153, Australia
Manufactured in the United States of America

Sterling ISBN 0-8069-9511-4

CONTENTS

RECIPES

TRADITIONAL BREADS 99

PREFACE

My first three bread books, *Great Bread Machine Recipes, Quick and Delicious Bread Machine Recipes,* and *Favorite Bread Machine Recipes,* had such excellent responses that I continued to develop new recipes. I tried hard to develop recipes that would be interesting, somewhat unusual, healthy, and fun to prepare. My goal was to make the use of the bread machine fun, educational, and, above all, to make bread that was tasty. The result was this fourth book of recipes.

All of the recipes in this book are original creations, with ideas coming from various sources, including family recipe files, friends, associates, standard bread recipes, the Internet, and even cereal boxes. Since "normal" bread recipes vary greatly in size, texture, and ingredients, all must be subjected to a conversion process in order to work in the bread machine. The result is rarely identical to the original recipe. In fact, every recipe in this book has been subjected to a rigorous process of conversion and experimentation. Let me explain how I learned to do this and how you, too, can convert your favorite "normal" bread recipes so that you can use them in your bread machine.

After I bought my first bread machine and overcame my initial fear of experimenting with it, I began to record the good recipes and make notes on the bad ones for future reference. Once I figured out how the machine worked, I wrote some computer software to assist me in developing recipes. The software helped me experiment and have fewer failures, and I began to formulate a set of parameters for bread machines recipes that, when adhered to, would usually yield good results.

The recipes in this book are the result of several years of this work and experimentation. As you will see, these recipes vary greatly and use different types of grains, flours, seeds, and other ingredients. Trying different kinds of breads is an exciting and tantalizing activity, particularly for bread lovers. In addition, it gives you total control over what you eat. In these times of heightened health consciousness, knowing what we are eating is a high priority.

These breads contain only natural ingredients. With a bread machine, you can select recipes that not only appeal to your palate, but give you the nutritional boost you are seeking. Diets need not eliminate bread, as long as you can produce wholesome bread with few empty calories. In fact, many diets promote bread because bread—particularly homemade bread—is full of grains and rich in nutrients. Because we are all sensitive to what we are eating, I have calculated the nutritional values for each of the loaves of bread in this book. This book features an expanded ingredient list in light of the fact that, over the years, consumers have become much more conscious of their food intake.

There are many bread machines on the market, and not all will bake the same. The machines vary in their motor size, baking capacity, cycle types and lengths, baking options, and appearance. In the past two years, many new types of machines have hit the market en masse. They are more affordable and feature-rich than ever before. In testing recipes on different machines, I have found considerable variation in the quality of the bread produced by the different machines. All of the recipes in this book were tested on an older Hitachi machine (without many of the bells and whistles found on newer machines), and I have presented the recipes here as they worked in that machine. Each machine is unique, and you may have to make slight modifications for yours. In general, where your machine calls for all of the ingredients to be placed in the bucket at one time, the recipes in this book will work unchanged. I have made no attempt to survey the unique characteristics of the many machines on the market, nor to make modifications specific to those.

Feel free to experiment. The freedom of experimentation allowed me to develop most of the recipes in this book, and you can do the same. Once you become familiar with the basic ingredients of bread, you will be able to make substitutions, convert old "normal" bread recipes, and even invent your own creations. Many of the breads in this book began as standard recipes and evolved through experimentation; they capture the essence of the original bread while working well in the bread machine.

Consider these recipes as a beginning, and make your own notes in the margins of this book. Watch the machine work. Become familiar with its sounds, the texture of the doughs, and its cycles. Familiarity with your machine will lead to the desire to strike out on your own to try new and wonderful tastes in bread. Happy baking!

Acknowledgments

Without the assistance and encouragement of numerous people, this book would not have been possible. I would like to thank readers of my first three books for their letters and comments, which encouraged me to continue with this fourth effort. Additionally, I want to thank my wife, Margie, for doing much of the research that was involved in this project. I would also like to thank the personnel at Sterling Publishing for their faith in this project, attention to detail in the handling of the manuscript, and their patience as I missed deadlines.

GETTING TO KNOW YOUR BREAD MAKER

Basic Operations

Although bread machines come in various shapes, sizes, capacities, and capabilities, they all share common characteristics and principles of operation. They are all designed to make bread making easy, quick, and complete. Except for placing the proper ingredients in the baking pan, pressing a few buttons, and removing the bread when it is finished (and slicing it, of course), the machine does all the work.

After ingredients are placed in the pan and you start the machine, the following cycles are completed:

1. The initial mix cycle

2. The first rise

3. The "punch down"

4. The second rise

5. The bake

6. The cool down

The length of each cycle depends on the make and model of your machine. Some machines skip the second rise and bake after the first rise. Other machines have alternate settings that let you select a double or single rise (often called the "quick bread" cycle). Some of the new machines have cycles especially created for whole grain breads, which generally require longer rising cycles. In addition, some machines have added capabilities, such as special cycles for cooking rice, jam, quick breads (batter breads), and cakes.

Whatever your machine's configuration, you need to become familiar with the way it works so you can tap its full potential for making delicious loaves of bread.

Capacities and Limitations

Each machine has a maximum capacity and limitation. Capacities are usually either 1 pound or 1½ pounds, with a few machines accommodating loaf sizes of 2 pounds. It is not wise to exceed the rated capacity of your machine, because overloading the machine can cause motor damage or dough overflows.

I have seen ads for machines that can bake "3 pound loaves," but the fine print will usually reveal that this will only work in the case of a dense bread that doesn't rise much. I would not recommend baking loaves much larger than your machine can handle, as it could cause damage to your machine, particularly the mixing motor.

What about baking a loaf smaller than the rated capacity? On most machines, that will work fine. The recipes in this book are presented in 1 pound, 1½ pound, and 2 pound sizes. If you have a 1 pound machine, limit yourself to baking the 1 pound loaves. If you have a larger, 1½ pound machine, feel free to try both 1 and 1½ pound recipe sizes.

Table 1 shows the basic capacity differences among bread machines currently on the market. You can determine the capacity of your machine from the owner's manual or determine the capacity by checking the white bread recipe that came with the machine. If the recipe calls for 2 cups of bread flour, you have a 1 pound machine. If it calls for 3 or more cups, you have a 1½ pound (or greater) capacity machine.

Table 1. Bread Machine Capacities: Basic White Bread Recipe

Flour Amount	1 lb	1½ lb	1½+ lb
2 cups	X		
2.5 cups	X		
3 cups		X	
3.5 cups			X
3 to 4 cups			X

Note: Determine the amount of flour called for in the basic white bread recipe for your machine. This chart will tell you the capacity of your machine based on that amount. If you do not have access to the basic white bread recipe that came with your machine, assume that it has a 1 pound capacity.

Baking the Dough Yourself

All machines let you bake the dough yourself in the oven by extracting it from the machine after the first rise is complete. If your machine has a dough setting, it will beep when it is time to remove the dough. You can then punch the dough down, knead it, place it in a bread pan or on a cookie sheet for a final rise, and bake in an oven, rather than in the machine itself.

Adding Ingredients

Some machines have a "mix bread" setting, which will beep when it is time to add raisins, seeds, or other ingredients to the dough. Since not all machines have this capability, I have developed the recipes in this book so all ingredients can be placed in the pan in the beginning. However, if you have a "mix" cycle, you can alternatively use that cycle, particularly in the recipes calling for seeds, nuts, or raisins. The advantage to adding these ingredients in a mix cycle is that the machine will tend to pound them less in the mixing process. Raisins, for example, will be more likely to remain whole when added in the mix bread cycle.

The timing of rising cycles varies somewhat from machine to machine. Some of the newer machines have separate cycles for whole wheat bread, which extends the rising time for the bread, giving a better rising loaf. Still other machines are programmable, allowing you to determine rise time yourself.

Crusts

The baking times vary on bread machines. Most machines offer you the option of selecting the darkness of your crust. The control for this will usually determine the baking temperature of your bread, and will not alter the length of the baking cycle. Selecting darker crusts will cause the bread to bake hotter. I found when using one machine, for example, that turning the dial to the lightest crust setting actually caused some breads to have uncooked dough in the middle. It will probably take a few loaves for you to determine the optimum setting to accommodate both your machine's capabilities and your personal tastes. Once you determine that setting, make a note of it, because you will probably want to bake all of your loaves with that same setting.

Knowing Your Own Machine

You will need to get used to your particular machine. In testing for my books I have found considerable variations among the different machines I have used. You will need to become familiar with two parts of the baking process as they apply to your specific machine: the optimum consistency of your dough and the sound of your machine as it goes through the cycles.

Dough Consistency

Dough consistency, and each machine's ability to deal with different dough consistencies, is important and varies greatly. Some machines will use a runnier dough (more liquid content); others have powerful motors that can easily handle stiffer doughs. Observe your bread as it is mixed. Make a mental note of the dough consistency. Then, when the bread is finished, note the texture of the bread. Learn to compare the finished texture to the consistency of the dough. Soon, you will be able to accurately predict the texture of the bread by looking at the dough immediately after mixing. This skill is important if you want to make any recipe modifications.

Machine Sounds

As you use your machine, also note the typical sounds it makes as it progresses through its various cycles. If you become familiar with the "normal" sounds, you will be aware when the motor is being overworked and the sounds the machine is making are unusual, which may indicate a process is potentially damaging.

Service and Cleaning

Cleaning

If you want consistently good bread from your machine, make sure it remains clean. Taking two or three minutes after each loaf has baked to clean the machine will yield consistently better loaves and will assure that your machine stays in peak operating condition.

How hard a machine is to clean depends on its design. Some machines use a bucket with the beater drive mechanism built in. Consequently, cleaning is simply a matter of removing the bread from the bucket, removing the beater, and cleaning the bucket with warm water. On other machines, the beater drive mechanism is not part of the bucket and must be cleaned after each use. This cleaning is more difficult and sometimes results in crumbs in the bottom of the baking chamber. To clean crumbs from the baking chamber, I have found that a damp kitchen washcloth will pick up most of them. I have tried mini-vacuums, canned air, and other methods such as turning the whole unit upside down and shaking it, but I find the simple washcloth the best (and least messy).

All machines have a special nonstick surface in the bread pan. Take care with this surface. Do not use any abrasive cleaners or scouring pads on the inside of the bread pan, or you will damage the nonstick surface. Try not to pry stuck breads with knives, forks, or other hard objects that may scratch the surface. If you must pry, use a rubber or soft plastic device of some kind, like a rubber spatula. If you take care of your bread pan, it will give you many future loaves of bread.

The machines that have the beater mechanism designed into the housing, rather than the bread bucket, also have a small plastic washer. Take great care with this washer. Don't lose it, and rinse it off and dry it after each loaf of bread. Without this washer, you will not have a good seal between your bucket and the bottom of your baking chamber, and leakage will result.

If you have an accident with your bread (such as dough overflow or another big mess), wait until the machine cools down, and take your time cleaning it. Most baked-on bread can be removed with warm water, and that is the recommended cleanup. I have had my share of disasters, but have managed to clean all of them up without even having to use any soap. Simple warm water and a washcloth have always been all that is needed.

Lost and Damaged Parts

There are generally no user-serviceable components in the bread machine, other than the standard cleaning of the parts just mentioned. However, there are parts that are easily lost or damaged that you can replace yourself. Most prominent on that list is the mixer beater. Since it is a small, removable part, it is easily misplaced. Make sure that you replace the beater in the bucket after each cleaning; that will minimize its potential for being lost.

On machines in which a plastic washer fits beneath the bread bucket, the washer will wear out over time. It is important to keep it clean, and it might not be a bad idea to order a replacement to have on hand, since it is an inexpensive item.

Bread Pan

The other major removable component is the bread pan. The most likely place of damage is its nonstick surface. If its surface is damaged to the point where bread is sticking to it, replace the bread pan. If small scratches seem to have no negative effect on your being able to remove the bread from the pan, you have probably not damaged the surface enough to worry about it.

Major Repairs

If any other problems arise with your machine, it is likely it will have to be sent in for repair. The control panel, for example, will sometimes cease to function and will need to be replaced. You should obtain an estimate of repairs before authorizing any major repairs on your machine because it is possible that the cost of repairs will exceed the cost of the machine, especially since the price of new machines will continue to fall for the foreseeable future as manufacturers achieve economy of scale. The likelihood is that your machine will have a long, productive life, and that it will give you many hours of trouble-free bread baking if you will simply keep it clean and ready for the next loaf.

Troubleshooting Guide

There are numerous variables that can affect your bread. Those listed below are all problems I have experienced while making bread in my bread machines. You may also encounter some not listed here. Before you write off the bread machine completely, send it out to repair, or blame the recipe, think the problem through and make sure that you have accounted for all other possible reasons for the problem. That would include crust settings, proper baking cycles, measuring ingredients properly, using fresh ingredients, checking for power outages during baking (which may recycle your machine), and, finally, curious children pushing buttons.

Stuck Dough Beater

If your dough beater is difficult to remove after baking a loaf of bread, try using some shortening on the shaft before installing the beater, and place dry ingredients in the pan first. In the machines where the beater is self-contained in the pan, soak the beater in water for a few minutes after removing the bread. In some types of machines, the beater will stay with the loaf of bread. In those types of machines, the beater is rarely a problem to remove.

Leakage of Liquid

This might be a problem on the machines whose pans have a hole in the bottom to accommodate the dough beater. If you have this kind of machine, place the dry ingredients in the bread pan first. Liquids should be added last. Also, check to make sure you have the rubber sealing washer in the proper position before locking the pan in place, and then make sure the pan is securely locked before adding ingredients.

Recipe Flop

Make sure you have added the proper quantities of ingredients. It is easy to become distracted while setting up a recipe and miscount your ingredients. Also, check to make sure you chose the correct settings when baking the bread. Finally, be sure your ingredients are fresh and that the proper type of ingredient has been used. A frequent culprit in recipe flops is yeast that is not fresh.

Loaf-Size Variation

The size of your loaf will vary according to the ingredients. Although the weight of two loaves of bread may be the same, their size and appearance may vary greatly. This is due to the different ingredients used. In general, breads using gluten-rich bread flour will rise more than breads using flours with less gluten content. Rye breads, for example, will be small, with dense texture, and will bake with a darker crust. The loaf sizes of the recipes in this book refer to weight, not to finished size.

Spoiled Ingredients

The two ingredients you must be cautious with are fresh eggs and fresh milk. Do not use either of these ingredients in a "delay bake" cycle (available on some machines), where you set the timer to start the bread at a later time. Milk would be all right if the delay were not more than an hour or two, but I would not recommend that eggs be used in any recipe that will not immediately be started. If you want to use a recipe calling for eggs on a delay bake, consider using powdered eggs instead of fresh eggs. If you want to use milk in a delayed recipe, use dry milk and add the proper amount of water to compensate.

Collapsing Dough

If your dough collapses, it dough probably rose too long. Since the timer cycles are not programmable on many machines, you may consider reducing the yeast by ½ teaspoon to get less rising. You also should check to make sure that the machine was not recycled during the process. Recycling can occur from brief power outages, or from children (or curious adults) pressing machine buttons. If a power outage occurs and you are aware of it, you can remove the dough from the machine and finish the process by hand, baking the bread in the oven. If your machine is programmable, set the rise cycle for a shorter time the next time you bake that recipe.

Strong Yeast Flavor
It is possible that too much yeast was added. Cut the yeast down by ½ teaspoon and try again.

Failure to Rise
This can be a complex problem with many possible causes. Any of the following will contribute to a loaf not properly rising:

• Using flour with low gluten content (pure rye flour, wheat flour, etc.)

• Too much salt in the recipe. Salt is a yeast inhibitor.

• Too little sugar in the recipe. Sugar feeds yeast and promotes rising.

• Yeast is old. Yeast expires. Check your yeast supply and make sure you are using fresh yeast. Old yeast will not activate and rise properly.

• Yeast is dead. This may be caused by adding hot ingredients. For example, if your recipe calls for some ingredients to be boiled before being added to the mix, do not add them until they have had time to cool. Adding ingredients that are too hot will kill your yeast.

Uneven Top
This usually indicates too little liquid in the recipe, but on some breads, such as rye breads, where less rising takes place, this may be a normal occurrence.

Collapsed Top
This is usually caused by too much liquid in the recipe. Cut the liquid back by two tablespoons and try again. Be careful not to make your bread dough too stiff, however, as some machines have underpowered motors that will not be able to handle stiffer dough, particularly in the 1½ pound recipes. Also be aware that some recipes use ingredients that are going to add liquid to the dough during the baking cycle, and a collapsed top might be nor-

mal. I found that breads using fresh cheeses generally fall into this category.

Rancid Taste

Check your whole grain ingredients. Whole grain flours, wheat germ, and similar ingredients should be kept in the freezer. They spoil rapidly when left at room temperature. White flours are not subject to the same type of spoilage and can be left in the cupboard for storage.

White Spots

These are from flour that has stuck to the side of the pan during the mixing process and has not mixed into the dough. This problem seems to occur more frequently in square pans than in round ones. When the bread rises and bakes, this flour sticks to the outside of the loaf. While not a taste problem, spots can present a cosmetic problem. The solution is to look into the baking pan after the mixing has taken place. If there is flour stuck to the sides of the pan, take a rubber spatula, remove it from the sides, and mix it in with the dough.

Soggy Crust

You left the bread in the pan too long after the baking cycle completed. Some machines have cooling cycles that cool the bread and help remove the moisture. Soggy crust is not as great a problem on these machines, but it is still a good idea to remove the bread and place it on a cooling rack as soon as the final beep is heard.

Improper Mix

This happened to me one time when I had forgotten to replace the dough beater after cleanup from the previous loaf. My solution to this is now to watch the initial mix for a minute or so when I first turn the machine on. I can see the mixing taking place. If the motor is running, but no mixing is happening, check your dough beater. If it has been left out, stop the machine, replace the beater, and start the cycle over.

Inconsistent Size and Texture

If you bake the same recipe and get different results, blame the weather. Weather is actually a large factor in baking, as temperature and humidity have substantial control over the amount of dough rising that will take place. Make notes as you bake and you will soon learn to make seasonal adjustments for your particular climate.

Lost Dough Beater

Check the last loaf of bread, particularly if your machine is of the variety where the beater stays in the loaf of bread when it is removed from the baking pan. I had a loaf of bread ready to give to a friend for testing, only to realize that I was about to give away the dough beater too! Get in the habit of cleaning your pan right away and putting everything back in the machine, and your beater will always be where you want it: In the pan, ready to bake.

CONVERTING EXISTING RECIPES

After you have had time to get used to your bread machine, you will probably want to try out some of your favorite bread recipes. When you look at them, however, you will notice that they were not designed to work in a bread machine. Practically any yeast bread recipe can be converted to work in your bread machine as long as you want to go to the effort of making the conversion. The key is to make sure the recipe is yeast-based. Although today we enjoy yeast which is reliable and easy to use, this is a relatively recent development. Recipes that are over 40 or 50 years old will likely use a chemical, rather than an organic, leavening. Chemical leavenings include baking soda and baking powder, and they do not have the same properties as yeast. Do not attempt to convert recipes that are not yeast-based for use in your bread machine.

Some machines have a cycle for "quick breads." These cycles are specifically designed for non-yeast baking (in fact, some of the machines can bake cake too!). Often called "batter breads," quick breads are breads that use batter with a consistency similar to pancake batter or cake batter. Quick breads are raised by means other than yeast. However, since most bread machines do not have these cycles, discussions regarding quick bread recipes are really beyond the scope of this book. We will stick to only yeast breads here.

Converting a standard bread recipe to work in your machine is not difficult, but is computationally intensive work, so have a calculator handy if you want to attempt a conversion. A sheet or two of paper will also be necessary, so you can write down the totals and the new, converted recipe.

This chapter will take you through the steps for converting a "regular" (non-machine) recipe to one you can try in your machine. It may take one or two trials to perfect the recipe, but the chances are good that you can successfully make the conversion. Before converting a recipe, make sure that it is a yeast bread recipe. As mentioned above, most bread machines are not designed to handle batter breads or breads using chemically based leavenings such as baking powder and baking soda.

Basic Steps

The four basic steps to convert a recipe are:

1. Cut the recipe down so it will make one loaf. Many recipes are designed to make two loaves and you will need to cut these in half because you will need a single-loaf recipe.

2. Determine the parameters of your particular bread machine.

3. Determine the liquidity ratio of the recipe. This is the "stiffness" of the dough. This is important because your machine has a rather narrow range of doughs it can handle.

4. Determine the overall bulk of the recipe. You do not want a recipe that is too large for your machine.

Let's look at each of these steps in turn, with particular attention to the details involved in each step. Once you have accomplished a few conversions, you will no longer need to refer to this book because the steps are not really so complex as they might seem at first.

Step One: Reduce the Recipe Size

Most recipes will tell you how many loaves they make. Some will even tell you the approximate size of each loaf. Cut the recipe down so it will make one loaf. This may involve some calculations on your part, so a good technique is to write down the new recipe as you reduce it from the original.

If the recipe doesn't say how many loaves it makes, you can make a rough judgment by looking at the amount of flour required. A one-pound loaf of bread will require about two cups of flour. Thus, if your recipe calls for six cups of all-purpose flour, you can probably figure that it will make three 1-pound loaves, or two 1½-pound loaves, or three 2-pound loaves.

Step Two: Determine the Parameters of Your Machine

Since each machine varies in its capacity and motor power, you must determine the acceptable ranges for your machine in two categories: liquidity ratio and bulk. Table 2 shows the acceptable liquidity ratio ranges. To find your machine's range, look at the basic white bread recipe that came with the machine. Determine the number of cups of flour called for, and follow that column until you find the row that shows the number of ounces of liquid (water or milk) called for in the recipe. In that box you will find the ratio range for your machine. Highlight or write down that ratio range (see page 126, where you can write down information about your bread machine.)

Bulk is also simply calculated by determining the number of cups of flour called for in the basic white bread recipe for your machine. If the recipe calls for 2-2½ cups of flour, you have a 1-pound machine. If the recipe calls for 3-4 cups of flour, you have a 1½ pound (or greater) machine.

Once you have written this information down, you will, in the future, be able to skip this step and move right from step one to step three.

Table 2. Bread Machine Liquidity Ratios

oz liq.	Cups of Flour			
	2 C*	2½ C	3 C	3½ C
5	2.9–3.5	3.6–4.4	4.3–5.3	5.0–6.2
6	**2.4–3.0**	3.0–3.6	3.6–4.4	4.2–5.2
7	**2.1–2.5**	2.6–3.2	3.1–3.7	3.6–4.4
8	1.8–2.2	2.3–2.8	2.7–3.3	3.2–3.9
9	1.6–2.0	2.0–2.4	**2.4–3.0**	2.8–3.4
10	1.4–1.8	1.8–2.2	**2.2–2.6**	2.5–3.1
11	1.4–1.7	1.6–2.0	2.0–2.4	2.3–2.8

Notes: *1 C (1 cup) = 8 ounces. Underlined entries show the most common bread machine ratio ranges. The ratio is computed by dividing dry ingredients by liquid ingredients. Higher ratios indicate stiffer dough; lower ratios indicate more liquid dough.

Step Three: Determine the Liquidity Ratio

Now you must determine the liquidity ratio (dough stiffness) of the recipe you are trying to convert. Table 3 (page 26) is a handy chart that you can duplicate and use each time you convert a recipe. To use the chart, simply fill in the ingredients and the amount called for in the original recipe. Write the amount in decimals (so your calculator can add them later) in the appropriate column. For example, if the recipe calls for 2½ cups of flour, enter 2.5 in the DRY Cup column. You will have to make a judgment as to whether the ingredient is dry or wet. In general, use the form that the ingredient is in when you add it. An exception to this would be an ingredient that is going to melt when heat is applied. They are considered liquids. Typical ingredients in this category would include butter, margarine, fresh cheeses, and shortening.

Some ingredients should not be computed. Do not include the following ingredients in the calculation:

1. Yeast

2. Raisins or nuts added at the mix cycle

3. Seeds added at the mix cycle

You should count raisins, nuts and seeds added initially as dry ingredients. The general rule is that if the ingredient will add to the stiffness of the dough, count it as a dry ingredient.

After you have entered all the ingredients, total each column and place the sum in the subtotal box. Then multiply each subtotal by the multiplier specified and place the result in the total box. Add the totals for dry ingredients together for a grand total (in teaspoons) and do the same for wet ingredients. Finally, divide the dry grand total by the wet grand total to compute the ratio for this recipe.

For best results, the ratio should fall within the liquidity ratio range designation for your machine (see step 2). If it only misses by a few points, it will probably be satisfactory. If the ratio for the recipe is below the range, your dough might be too wet. Try a slight reduction in liquid ingredients or an increase in dry ingredients and recalculate. If the ratio is above the range, it is too dry. Either reduce the dry ingredients slightly, or add liquid.

Chances are, you will still need to experiment to get the recipe just right, but this calculation will give you a good start and place you well beyond the "trial and error" stage.

Step Four: Determine the Overall Bulk
You certainly do not want to overflow your machine with your test recipe, so make sure the bulk does not exceed the capacity of your machine. If you have a 1 pound machine, you should make sure your recipe does not call for more than 2½ cups of flour. If you have a 1½ pound machine, 3½ to 3¾ cups of flour are about the limit. For a 2 pound machine, 4 to 5 cups would be the limit. If you need to adjust the recipe, make sure you make equal adjustments of wet and dry ingredients to maintain the liquidity ratio of the recipe.

Improving and Tailoring Your Recipes

After your initial attempt at your newly converted recipe, you may want to adjust the recipe to increase or decrease bulk, reduce or increase rise, or alter texture or taste. Experiment with the recipe until you have perfected it. Part of the enjoyment of a bread machine is being able to try new and exciting recipes and to be creative. Although the conversion process, as presented here, may seem somewhat better suited to a mathematician than an artist, science and art go hand in hand in bread baking. Once you get to know your machine and your ingredients, you will feel comfortable making substitutions, or even trying brand new creations, made from scratch.

Table 3. Dough Liquidity Calculation Worksheet

Ingredient	DRY			WET			
	t	T	C	t	T	C	oz
Subtotal							
Multiplier		3	4^8		3	4^8	6
TOTAL							
GRAND TOTAL							
Liquidity Ratio							

Instructions: 1. Use decimals for fractions (.5 teaspoon, etc.). 2. Subtotal each column. 3. Multiply the subtotal by the multiplier to obtain the total. Add the dry totals and the wet totals separately to obtain the wet and dry grand totals. 5. Divide the dry grand total by the wet grand total to get the liquidity ratio.

RECIPE POINTERS

Recipe Sizes

Three sizes are given for each of the recipes in this book, although smaller, and some larger, sizes are possible. I found in experimenting with a possible ¾ pound size loaf that the machines tended to overbake the small loaves, and that they typically were too dry. Consequently, I decided to present here only the three sizes that will be accommodated by virtually all bread machines.

Recipe sizes refer to finished weight, not dimensions. The finished dimensions of the bread will depend to a great extent on baking conditions, amounts of yeast used, and types of ingredients. A 1-pound loaf of white bread, for example, might be larger than a 1½-pound loaf of rye bread, which tends to be more densely textured.

Modifications for Specific Machines

I have tried to include recipes that will work in any machine. On the 1-pound recipes, I found virtually no difference when testing the recipes in different machines. With the larger loaves, however, I noticed that some machines will not tolerate a stiff dough as well as others. If your machine's motor seems to be laboring with a certain dough, you might consider adding an extra tablespoon or two tablespoons more liquid. This will lower the liquidity ratio slightly, making the dough less stiff. As mentioned previously, you will come to recognize the "normal" sounds of your machine and will be able to identify those situations when slight recipe modifications are needed.

The other major difference between machines is in their rise cycles and the amount of yeast called for. I have tried to optimize the amount of yeast in the recipes to be suitable to all machines. If your machine has a dispenser or other device that causes a change in the amount of yeast normally used, you should make the modification to the amount of yeast in the recipe.

Many machines have "rapid bread" cycles that allow you to bake a loaf faster (single rise, rather than the usual double rise). When using the rapid bread cycle on your machine, double the amount of yeast that is normally called for, or consult your owner's manual for the proper yeast adjustment.

Ingredients

There is a wide variety of ingredients called for in these recipes. Many are available at your local supermarket, but some must be purchased at health food stores. Some mail order sources are available if you do not have a health food store nearby. Here is a summary of important information about some of the main ingredients used in the recipes in this book.

White Flours

All wheat-based flours are made from various combinations of three different varieties of wheat: hard wheat, soft wheat, and durum wheat. Of the three, hard wheat is highest in protein content and best for bread-making. Soft wheat makes finer flour with less protein content. Durum wheat is used for semolina flour, which is a high-protein flour specifically used for pasta making. Flours vary by the combination of these wheat types used.

There are two main types of white flours, *all-purpose flour* and *bread flour*. All-purpose flour is made from about 80% hard wheat and 20% soft wheat. Bread flour is made from 100% hard wheat, giving it slightly better breadmaking characteristics. Both varieties are available in most grocery stores. Bread flour is slightly higher in gluten content than all-purpose flour and will usually rise more. You should try to use the type of flour called for in the recipe. Substituting all-purpose flour for bread flour is permissible; however, it may slightly change the texture of the bread and cause it to rise less.

You will also note that all-purpose flour is available both in *bleached* and *unbleached* varieties. Bleached flour is treated during the milling process with chlorine, which shortens the processing time in whitening the flour. Unbleached flour is refined without the chlorination, but takes longer to process as a result, and will generally cost more. If the process has been speeded up by the addition of a chemical called bromate, the flour will be labeled as "bromated" flour.

On supermarket shelves you will often see pastry flour, cake flour, and self-rising flours. Pastry flour and cake flour are very finely ground flours and are made from 100% soft wheat. They are not suitable for breadmaking. Self-rising flour contains salt and baking soda and is not useful for breadmaking either.

Whole Grains

Whole Wheat Flour: This flour is ground from the complete wheat berry and contains the wheat germ and the wheat bran. It is coarser and heavier than white flour, and does not rise as much. I purchase fresh wheat in bulk and grind it myself for the best-tasting bread; however, this may be more than most people can do. Grocery stores carry whole wheat flour, usually right alongside the white flour.

Graham Flour: In the early 20th century, Sylvester Graham publicly argued the merits of grains in the diet, wheat in particular. Graham flour is essentially equivalent to whole wheat flour, except that the milling process varies somewhat, with a slightly coarser grind and larger particles of bran throughout. This gives it a sweeter flavor than whole wheat flour. In recipes calling for graham flour, you may freely substitute whole wheat flour if graham flour is not available.

Semolina Flour: This is whole grain durum wheat with the bran layer removed. It can be used for breadmaking, particularly when used in combination with bread flour.

Bran: Bran is the outer covering of the kernel of wheat or oat. It is rich in fiber and is called for in small quantities in some recipes. Recently, much has been said about the benefits of oat bran. Both oat and wheat bran are available at most grocery stores.

Wheat Germ: This part of the wheat grain is readily available in grocery stores. Like bran, it is used sparingly in recipes. Wheat germ should be kept in the refrigerator after the container is opened.

Gluten Flour: Gluten is a protein found in the wheat berry. Gluten is necessary for rising to occur. When mixed with water, it forms an elastic substance that catches the gas bubbles formed by the leavening agent. Flours made from wheat, including whole wheat flour, white flour, and bread flour, contain plenty of gluten, but some whole grain flours do not. I have found that some gluten flour added to the mix when using a low-gluten flour will make for better rising and texture. Gluten flour can be purchased at any good health food store. A few recipes call for gluten flour, but most make it optional. Some people are allergic to gluten. Those individuals should stick to low-gluten flours, including rye and quinoa.

Rye Flour: This flour is very low in gluten content, so it will not rise when used by itself. Most of the recipes in this book call for a mixture of rye and another flour with a higher gluten content. This will let the bread rise.

Barley Flour: Barley flour lends a sweet taste and smooth texture to bread. Most recipes call for it in combination with white or wheat flour, since it has no gluten content. You will probably have to go to a health food store to find barley flour.

Buckwheat: Buckwheat is a strong-tasting flour for which some aficionados have acquired a real taste. In spite of its name, it is not made from wheat. Buckwheat is actually a grass, which yields groats, which can then be ground into flour. It is usually used in somewhat small quantities, but if you develop a liking for the strong flavor it presents, you can use it in combination with whole wheat flour. Called *kasha* in some parts of the world.

Cracked Wheat: As its name implies, this is part of the wheat berry. It is very hard and usually requires some soaking before use. It is widely available at health food stores and can often also be found in grocery stores.

7-Grain Cereal: This cereal has an appearance similar to cracked wheat, but consists of seven grains, including wheat, barley, corn, and oats. It is available at health food stores.

Oats: Use rolled oats (oatmeal) for your oat recipes. Just use the type available at the grocery store. When measuring rolled oats, pack them down into the measuring cup to get a full measure.

Oat Flour: This is flour ground specifically for bread from the oat groats. Since it has no gluten content, it has to be used in combination with a wheat flour of some kind.

Quinoa: This flour is imported from South America; it was a staple grain of the Incas in ancient times. It has one of the highest protein contents of any grain, and gives bread a somewhat nutty flavor.

Soy Flour: This flour is ground from soybeans; it is high in protein content at about 40–50%. It is very nutritious, but not flavorful, and is often used as an ingredient for enriching the nutritional value of bread.

Millet: This is a small, yellow, perfectly round grain. It can be used in bread whole, raw or cooked, or milled into flour.

Rice: Rice, a staple throughout the world, can be cooked and added to bread, or made into flour. The flour absorbs moisture more slowly than most flours, so it is well known among bakers as an excellent flour for dusting breads and pizza.

Liquids

Water is called for in most recipes. It should be used warm (between 100 and 110°F (37.8 to 43.3°C). I have found that hot tap water works fine. Don't heat the water any further, because water that is too hot can kill the yeast.

Milk: When milk is called for in a recipe, I use 1% or skim milk. In fact, the nutritional counts in the recipes in this book are calculated using values for 1% milk. If you do not have milk on hand, try using dry milk and adding the requisite amount of water to the recipe. Milk should usually be warmed to 100 to 110°F (37.8 to 43.3°C); the microwave works well for this at 45 seconds on high. Be careful not to overheat the milk, or you will kill the yeast.

Buttermilk: You can use buttermilk in its fresh form, or purchase buttermilk powder to mix it as needed. I do the latter, since I don't particularly like to drink buttermilk, and since recipes usually call for only small amounts. In most recipes, it is safe to substitute low-fat or skim milk for buttermilk. You may sacrifice some flavor, but it will be result in a lower fat content for your bread.

Cream: There are several types of cream available at most grocery stores: heavy cream, light cream, whipping cream, and half-and-half. Some recipes call for heavy or light cream, but I have found that whipping cream works fine in most cases where cream is called for. Note that *whipping cream* and *whipped cream* are different. Whipped cream has had sugar added and is already in whipped form. Whipping cream comes in a carton and pours like milk.

Eggs: Most of the recipes in this book have been formulated to call for whole eggs, rather than portions of eggs or egg whites only. However, if you are concerned about the cholesterol in eggs, you may freely substitute any commercially available egg substitute. Use ¼ cup (4 tablespoons) of egg substitute instead of each whole egg. You also may use powdered eggs, ¼ cup of mixed eggs instead of each whole egg.

Butter: Many of the recipes in this book call for butter. You may substitute margarine or vegetable oil in the same quantities for butter. Butter, however, will provide the most flavor. I keep my butter in the freezer because spoilage is the biggest problem with real butter. When I need butter, I remove it from the freezer, cut the required quantity from the cube, and replace the butter in the freezer. It takes only a few minutes for the portion of butter to get to room temperature,; then it can be placed in the bread pan. There is no need to melt butter or margarine before adding to the recipes, but it is best if the butter chunks are 1 tablespoon or smaller.

Olive Oil: I have used olive oil exclusively in these recipes, instead of calling for other oils. The taste is better and olive oil has no cholesterol. However, if you prefer another type of cooking oil, such as canola, corn oil, or any other vegetable oil, you may freely substitute. If you use olive oil, use a good grade of extra virgin olive oil.

Other Ingredients

Salt: Salt is a yeast inhibitor, and is necessary in most recipes. If you are on a salt-restricted diet, you can eliminate the salt from the recipes. You should know, however, that if you do so, the characteristics of the bread will change. The bread will rise differently; it may rise too much and then collapse. The resulting texture may also be different. Keep in mind that other ingredients often have salt content. If you are on a salt-restricted diet, check the nutritional values for each recipe to see if there are "hidden salts" in the recipe. Butter, for example, is one of the ingredients that has a sodium content. Avoid using salt substitutes as alternatives. They are chemically based and do not have the yeast inhibiting properties of real salt. They will do no good, and they may cause other chemical reactions that will change the properties of your bread.

Yeast: The recipes in this book call for yeast in teaspoons. I use active dry yeast, and I buy it in bulk. If kept in the refrigerator, it will last a long time. In fact, with my bread machine running, a supply of yeast doesn't last long at all. If you use cake yeast, you will need to make the conversion from teaspoons. If you purchase yeast in packets at the grocery store, one packet contains one scant tablespoon, or about 2¼ teaspoons of yeast. Do not use rapid rise yeast in these recipes.

Not all bread machines use the same amount of yeast in the large recipes. This is due to differences in cycle lengths and the yeast dispensing mechanisms available on a few machines. If a recipe does not rise enough, try adding an extra ½ teaspoon of yeast.

Yeast feeds on sugars and is inhibited by salts. It likes a warm environment, but too much heat will kill it. Most traditional bread recipes will require you to "proof" your yeast before using it. Proofing means mixing the yeast with sugar and warm (105 to 110°F, 40.6 to 43.3°C) water to allow it to become active before adding it to the recipe. Proofing is not necessary with bread machines; however, it is a good technique to use if you want to make sure your yeast is active (not too old). Yeast can be placed directly into the bread pan. When it touches liquid, it will begin to be active.

Sugars and Sweeteners: These are necessary in all bread recipes because they provide food for the yeast. Recipes in this book call for sugar (white, granulated), honey, syrup, molasses, or brown sugar. Molasses comes in various types, but I use blackstrap when baking. I have tried others, and haven't noticed any appreciable difference in the outcome, so use whatever molasses you happen to have on hand if a recipe calls for it. By the way, if the recipe calls for olive oil and honey or molasses, measure the olive oil first and don't rinse the spoon off. The honey or molasses will slide right out of the spoon into your pan!

Dough Enhancer: This product is difficult to find. Even health food stores may not carry it. You can find it at baking specialty stores or obtain it through mail order. Dough enhancer is a tofu (soybean) based powder that makes the dough smoother, and it is what commercial bakers often use to obtain the smooth-textured bread you buy at the store.

Spices, Nuts, and Seeds: These ingredients are called for in wide variety in recipes. I found most of the spices, seeds, and nuts called for in these recipes at the grocery store. If you cannot find them, you might try your health food store, which will usually stock some of the lesser known spices. Feel free to experiment with spices, adding more of spices you like and deleting those you do not. Often it is the blend of spices that makes the flavor, rather than any single spice, in those recipes calling for two or three different spices.

You will find that your spice cabinet enlarges as you bake more breads. Eventually, you will have a stock of almost any spice called for in a recipe. Preserving spices and seeds is not a problem, but preserving fresh nuts is. A few recipes call for fresh-chopped nuts. Use any type of nuts you enjoy, but keep in mind that nuts will go rancid if not used in a short period, so keep your supply of nuts fresh.

The Order of Ingredients

There are two ways to place ingredients in the baking pan: Dry ingredients first or wet ingredients first. Most machines call for wet ingredients first, so that order is used in this book. Actually, dry first will work in all machines, except when you want to use a timed bake function. In that case, you will not want to activate the yeast until the baking process starts, so wet ingredients will have to go first, with yeast last. The machines that recommend dry ingredients first call for yeast as the first ingredient, followed by the other dry ingredients and, finally, the liquids. If your machine calls for dry ingredients first, add the ingredients to the pan in reverse order from that listed here.

Preparation of Ingredients

Most bread recipes call for all ingredients to be at room temperature, except for liquids, which are sometimes called for at 105 to 110°F (40.6 to 43.3°C). I have experimented with this and have not had real problems adding refrigerated ingredients. Rather than worry too much about it, just try setting all of your ingredients out first and then adding them. Once you get to the refrigerated ingredients, they have usually approached room temperature anyway.

When warm water is called for, it should be in the 105 to 110°F (40.6 to 43.3°C) range. I used to use a thermometer to make sure that the water was the correct temperature; however, I soon gave up on that when I found that hot tap water usually approached that range. Hot tap water varies, however, so make sure that yours is not too hot (too hot presents a much bigger problem than too cold).

Milk can be measured and then left to reach room temperature, or you can use the microwave to warm it up. Just be sure that if you use the microwave, you don't overheat the milk, which is easy to do in the microwave. If you overheat it, let it sit until it cools to 110°F (43.3°C) or lower before adding it to the bread pan.

For measuring flour and dry ingredients, I use the dip-and-level method, rather than the spoon method. For the dip-and-level method, simply dip your measuring cup into the flour and level it with a knife or other flat edge.

Making Substitutions and Modifications

I would recommend that you try the recipes as given the first time. Then if you want to make substitutions or modifications, experiment all you want. I have found that the best way to experiment is to alter one item at a time. If you alter too many things at once and the recipe fails, you will not be able to determine the cause of the failure. However, if you only altered one ingredient, you will know that the alteration was the only variable that could have caused failure.

You can freely make the substitutions mentioned in the ingredients section, including margarine for butter, low-fat or skim milk for buttermilk, egg substitutes for whole eggs, and all-purpose flour for bread flour. Keep in mind, however, that these substitutions will alter the original recipe somewhat and results will be different.

Avoid the use of chemically based substitutes, such as sugar and salt substitutes. These chemically based products may taste the same in coffee or soft drinks, but they break down differently from sodium or sugar in baking environments and will not work properly with yeast breads. It is better simply to eliminate salt, for example, than to use a salt substitute. Yeast feeds fine on sugar, but doesn't have much of a taste for artificial sweeteners.

Once you have gained a feel for a recipe, and for your machine, feel free to experiment. Most of the recipes in this book were developed that way, and you can have a lot of fun trying new and wonderful ideas. It is best to begin with established recipes and make successive alterations until you arrive at the perfect bread. Be sure and keep a log of your changes and the results. That way you can learn as you go and won't repeat mistakes. It also helps to have a basic understanding of the principles of baking with yeast, and of the characteristics of the ingredients you are using.

Slicing Your Bread

When you get that loaf out of the machine, it smells wonderful. In fact, it has probably filled the whole house with the unmistakable odor of baking bread! You may want to dig in and eat the whole loaf right on the spot. Of course, you can do that. There is nothing better than fresh, hot bread. However, if your aim is to slice the bread and keep it for a few days, or use it for tomorrow's breakfast or lunch, then you will need to slice it more carefully.

Bread is best sliced after it has had a chance to cool completely. It then regains some of its stiffness and is much easier to handle. Slicing hot bread is a bit like trying to slice jello. As you cut, the bread gives, and it is difficult to get a good, straight slice.

For best results, remove your bread from the machine as soon as the "all done" alarm sounds. Place it on a cooling rack and let it cool completely (probably an hour or so). Although many machines now include cooling cycles, they cannot completely cool the bread, because the bread is still in the pan, where moisture and heat are trapped.

To slice the bread, use a serrated knife designed especially for slicing bread. Use a sawing motion and let the knife do the work. Putting too much downward pressure on the bread will smash it down and will give you uneven slices.

I inherited a meat slicer and don't use it for meat at all, but I have found it to be a wonderful bread slicer. I just set the thickness and the serrated blade cuts right through my cool loaf. If you have a slicer and your loaf is too big for it (the Welbilt loaves are too big for mine), cut the loaf in half lengthwise, making two half rounds. Then slice each half loaf with your slicer.

Nutritional Values

I am convinced that much of the consumer motivation behind the boom in bread machines sales is due to a desire to eat healthier foods. Whole grain breads are wonderful sources of nutrients, have no chemical preservatives, and taste great.

Each recipe is followed by the nutritional values. The values are per loaf, so to obtain a serving value, estimate how many slices you will make from the loaf and divide the value by the number of slices in the loaf. The nutritional values are estimates only, and should not be construed as anything else. They were derived by using *MasterCook* software package. Each of the ingredients in the recipes was calculated and totaled for each size of loaf. Below is an explanation of some of the main values used.

Calories are total calories for a loaf.

Protein is measured in grams. You will not find breads to be high in protein content, but when taken with other foods (meats or legumes like beans) that are high in protein, a healthy combination is made.

Carbohydrates are also measured in grams. Carbohydrates, especially from whole grain sources, provide a good ratio of nutrients to calories (the opposite of "empty calories") and should constitute 45 to 48% of our daily intake of calories.

Fat is listed as total fat and saturated fat. We should try to reduce the amount of fats in our diet, and saturated fats should be avoided as much as possible. Government recommendations are that we limit our total calories from fat to 30% of our daily intake of calories, and limit saturated fat calories to only 10%. I have computed the percentage of calories from fat for each recipe, in addition to giving you the amount of total fat and saturated fat in grams. These breads are very healthy from the standpoint of percentage of calories from fats.

Cholesterol content is measured in milligrams. Cholesterol is only found in animal fats.

Sodium is measured for each recipe (in milligrams); it can derive not only from the salt added to the recipe, but from the sodium content of some other recipe ingredients. If you are on a low-sodium diet, you can reduce the salt content of the loaf, with the limitations discussed previously.

Fiber is important to a growing number of health-conscious individuals. The fiber content of each recipe is measured in grams. Fiber takes several forms, and so the figure given is a total figure that includes both dietary and crude fiber. Most nutritionists would recommend at least 25 grams of fiber per day in your diet.

Recipe Testing

Your strategy for testing recipes should be to try the 1-pound loaf first, even if you have a 1½ or 2 pound capacity machine. This offers three advantages:

1. You can make sure you like the taste and texture of the bread, while using a small quantity of ingredients for the first test.

2. You can make sure the bread works well in your machine with fewer ingredients at risk.

3. You can make sure that your particular baking conditions will not produce an oversize loaf, with little risk of a mess if they do.

Once you have tested a bread, make alterations to suit your taste, baking conditions, and machine. For example, you can increase or reduce yeast amounts, liquidity, substitute seeds or nuts, or make other ingredient substitutions. I would highly recommend, however, that you try the recipe once as given before making your own modifications. That gives you a basis upon which to make your changes and a point of reference, as discussed earlier. After that, be creative.

THE HISTORY OF BREAD

It is unclear where the wheat plant originated. Historians know that it was cultivated in southwestern Asia as early as 15,000 BC. In 1948, archeologists from the University of Chicago unearthed an Iraqi village, dated at about 6,700 BC, and found the berries from several types of wheat.

Over the centuries, it probably became obvious to early people, mostly nomadic hunters and gatherers, that the wheat plant could be cultivated. These early farmers also discovered that wheat could be stored and used as both food and seed for the next crop.

Early man probably chewed wheat berries, rather than grinding and baking them. Later, he learned to grind the wheat into flour and use it to make an early form of hot cereal or porridge. Eventually, he learned to bake the dough. This early bread was not leavened, and was probably a densely textured flat bread.

Around 3,000 BC, the Egyptians discovered how to make leavened bread. As leavening was developed, originally with the use of sourdough starters, wheat remained the grain of choice, since it had the best properties and cellular structure for rising. Egyptian traders spread the idea to Greece and Rome, where hundreds of varieties of bread were developed.

In medieval Europe, baker's guilds were developed, as baking bread became both an occupation and an art form.

Commercial bread, as we know it, is a relatively recent product. As late as the 1940s, most bread eaten in America was homemade. Today, millions of loaves of bread are baked daily in completely automated bakeries, but the quality of the bread has been somewhat compromised in the process, due to the addition of preservatives to lengthen shelf life and other time-saving manufacturing devices.

Today, the best bread is still homemade. Bread machines were developed to give you the best of both worlds: convenience and homemade quality. You can choose the type of bread you want, control the ingredients, and eat it fresh from the oven (or bread machine).

BASIC BREADS

The breads in this section are old favorites and basic breads that are fitting for any occasion. If you are new to bread machines, try the breads in this section first.

Air Bread

Based on a James Beard muffin recipe, modifications to the thick muffin batter yield this slightly sweet-tasting white bread, which is great toasted.

1 lb	1½ lb	2 lb
5 oz warm water	7½ oz warm water	10 oz warm water
2½ T butter	3½ T butter	⅓ C butter
1 egg	1 egg	2 eggs
2 C bread flour	3 C bread flour	4 C bread flour
¼ C nonfat dry milk	⅜ C nonfat dry milk	½ C nonfat dry milk
1½ T sugar	2½ T sugar	3 T sugar
1 t active dry yeast	1½ t active dry yeast	2 t active dry yeast

Nutritional Analysis (per loaf, approximate)

Item	1 lb	1½ lb	2 lb
total calories (kcal)	1496	2200	3026
total protein (g)	51	74	102
total carbohydrates (g)	235	356	470
total fat (g)	38	52	79
total saturated fat (g)	20	27	42
total cholesterol (mg)	263	297	536
total sodium (mg)	515	717	1069
total fiber (g)	8	12	15
% calories from fat	23	21	24

Basic White Bread

This basic white bread recipe should work in most bread machines and should give you good results. Use it as a gauge to tell how well your machine operates.

1 lb	1½ lb	2 lb
3 oz warm water	4½ oz warm water	6 oz warm water
3 oz milk	4½ oz milk	6 oz milk
1 T butter	1½ T butter	2 T butter
1 t salt	1½ t salt	2 t salt
2 C bread flour	3 C bread flour	4 C bread flour
2 T sugar	3 T sugar	¼ C sugar
½ t active dry yeast	1 t active dry yeast	1 t active dry yeast

Nutritional Analysis (per loaf, approximate)

Item	1 lb	1½ lb	2 lb
total calories (kcal)	1244	1870	2489
total protein (g)	37	55	73
total carbohydrates (g)	228	343	457
total fat (g)	19	28	38
total saturated fat (g)	10	14	19
total cholesterol (mg)	42	63	84
total sodium (mg)	2298	3448	4597
total fiber (g)	7	11	14
% calories from fat	14	14	14

Cornmeal Bread

This is a southwestern type bread that is excellent with a bowl of chili or a taco salad.

1 lb	1½ lb	2 lb
⅔ C milk	1 C milk	1⅓ C milk
½ C cottage cheese	¾ C cottage cheese	1 C cottage cheese
2 t dried onions	1 T dried onions	1⅓ T dried onions
1½ T green chili, diced	2 T green chili, diced	3 T green chili, diced
½ C cornmeal	⅔ C cornmeal	⅞ C cornmeal
2 t olive oil	1 T olive oil	1⅓ T olive oil
2 t sugar	1 T sugar	1⅓ T sugar
1¾ C bread flour	2⅔ C bread flour	3½ C bread flour
1 t active dry yeast	1½ t active dry yeast	2 t active dry yeast

Nutritional Analysis (per loaf, approximate)

Item	1 lb	1½ lb	2 lb
total calories (kcal)	1443	2164	2858
total protein (g)	57	86	114
total carbohydrates (g)	249	374	493
total fat (g)	22	33	44
total saturated fat (g)	7	10	14
total cholesterol (mg)	32	47	63
total sodium (mg)	549	823	1097
total fiber (g)	7	10	14
% calories from fat	14	14	14

Egg Bread

A staple white bread, simple to make and smooth in texture.

1 lb	1½ lb	2 lb
½ C milk	¾ C milk	1 C milk
2½ T butter	4 T butter	⅓ C butter
1 egg	1 egg	2 egg
½ t salt	¾ t salt	1 t salt
2 C bread flour	3 C bread flour	4 C bread flour
1 t active dry yeast	1½ active dry yeast	2 t active dry yeast

Nutritional Analysis (per loaf, approximate)

Item	1 lb	1½ lb	2 lb
total calories (kcal)	1390	2079	2814
total protein (g)	44	63	88
total carbohydrates (g)	207	310	413
total fat (g)	42	63	87
total saturated fat (g)	22	34	47
total cholesterol (mg)	274	328	558
total sodium (mg)	1476	2216	2990
total fiber (g)	8	12	15
% calories from fat	27	28	28

Egg Bread II

A slightly sweeter version of the previous Egg Bread recipe.

1 lb	1½ lb	2 lb
1 oz warm water	1½ oz warm water	2 oz warm water
3 T butter	¼ C butter	⅜ C butter
⅓ C milk	½ C milk	⅔ C milk
1 egg	1 egg	2 eggs
1 T sugar	1½ T sugar	2 T sugar
½ t salt	¾ t salt	1 t salt
2 C bread flour	3 C bread flour	4 C bread flour
1 t active dry yeast	1½ t active dry yeast	3 t active dry yeast

Nutritional Analysis (per loaf, approximate)

Item	1 lb	1½ lb	2 lb
total calories (kcal)	1464	2114	2927
total protein (g)	43	61	85
total carbohydrates (g)	217	325	434
total fat (g)	46	61	92
total saturated fat (g)	25	33	50
total cholesterol (mg)	284	320	567
total sodium (mg)	1515	2188	3030
total fiber (g)	8	12	15
% calories from fat	28	26	28

English Loaf

Breads don't come much simpler than this. The story is that an English food editor, Elizabeth David, developed this recipe when she became frustrated with the quality of the bread she was finding accompanying her gourmet meals. She developed this recipe to be simple, almost foolproof, and to have a wonderful aroma while baking and a slightly salty taste.

1 lb	1½ lb	2 lb
6 oz warm water	9 oz warm water	12 oz warm water
2 C bread flour	3 C bread flour	4 C bread flour
1 t salt	1½ t salt	2 t salt
1½ t active dry yeast	2¼ t active dry yeast	1 T active dry yeast

Nutritional Analysis (per loaf, approximate)			
Item	1 lb	1½ lb	2 lb
total calories (kcal)	1007	1510	2014
total protein (g)	35	53	70
total carbohydrates (g)	201	302	402
total fat (g)	5	7	10
total saturated fat (g)	1	1	1
total cholesterol (mg)	0	0	0
total sodium (mg)	2145	3218	4291
total fiber (g)	8	12	17
% calories from fat	4	4	4

Herb Bread

This bread makes excellent toast and has the hint of flavor from several different herbs, mixed together here in a wonderful combination.

1 lb	1½ lb	2 lb
3 oz milk	4½ oz milk	6 oz milk
1 T butter	1½ T butter	2 T butter
3 oz warm water	4½ oz warm water	6 oz warm water
1½ T sugar	2 T sugar	3 T sugar
1 t salt	1½ t salt	2 t salt
2 C whole wheat flour	3 C whole wheat flour	4 C whole wheat flour
½ each med. onions, chopped	¾ each med. onions, chopped	1 each med. onions, chopped
½ t dried dill weed	¾ t dried dill weed	1 t dried dill weed
½ t rosemary, crushed	¾ t rosemary, crushed	1 t rosemary, crushed
½ t basil	¾ t basil	1 t basil
1½ t active dry yeast	2¼ t active dry yeast	1 T active dry yeast

Nutritional Analysis (per loaf, approximate)

Item	1 lb	1½ lb	2 lb
total calories (kcal)	1072	1595	2143
total protein (g)	39	58	78
total carbohydrates (g)	202	300	405
total fat (g)	19	29	38
total saturated fat (g)	10	15	19
total cholesterol (mg)	42	63	84
total sodium (mg)	2504	3756	5009
total fiber (g)	32	48	64
% calories from fat	15	15	15

Honey Bread

A simple, somewhat sweet bread that is great eaten fresh and warm.

1 lb	1½ lb	2 lb
½ C milk	¾ C milk	1 C milk
3 T honey	¼ C honey	⅜ C honey
1½ T butter	2¼ T butter	3 T butter
½ t salt	¾ t salt	1 t salt
2 C bread flour	3 C bread flour	4 C bread flour
1½ t active dry yeast	2¼ t active dry yeast	1 T active dry yeast

Nutritional Analysis (per loaf, approximate)			
Item	1 lb	1½ lb	2 lb
total calories (kcal)	1426	2106	2851
total protein (g)	40	59	79
total carbohydrates (g)	259	380	518
total fat (g)	26	39	52
total saturated fat (g)	14	21	28
total cholesterol (mg)	63	94	125
total sodium (mg)	1310	1965	2620
total fiber (g)	8	13	17
% calories from fat	16	16	16

Honey French Bread

A sweeter version of traditional French bread, it's simple to make, has few ingredients, and is very low-fat.

1 lb	1½ lb	2 lb
2 t honey	1 T honey	1⅓ T honey
2 t olive oil	1 T olive oil	1⅓ T olive oil
¾ C warm water	9 oz warm water	1½ C warm water
2 C bread flour	3 C bread flour	4 C bread flour
1½ t salt	2¼ t salt	1 T salt
1 t sugar	1½ t sugar	2 t sugar

Nutritional Analysis (per loaf, approximate)

Item	1 lb	1½ lb	2 lb
total calories (kcal)	1128	1692	2256
total protein (g)	33	49	66
total carbohydrates (g)	215	322	429
total fat (g)	14	20	27
total saturated fat (g)	2	3	4
total cholesterol (mg)	0	0	0
total sodium (mg)	3209	4813	6418
total fiber (g)	1	2	2
% calories from fat	11	11	11

Honey Oatmeal Bread

A traditional oat bread, sweetened with a touch of honey.

1 lb	1½ lb	2 lb
1 T butter	1½ T butter	2 T butter
1½ T honey	2¼ T honey	3 T honey
¾ C warm water	9 oz warm water	1½ C warm water
¼ C rolled oats	⅜ C rolled oats	½ C rolled oats
¾ t salt	1¼ t salt	1½ t salt
2⅛ C bread flour	3¼ C bread flour	4½ C bread flour
1 t active dry yeast	1½ t active dry yeast	2 t active dry yeast

Nutritional Analysis (per loaf, approximate)

Item	1 lb	1½ lb	2 lb
total calories (kcal)	1338	2037	2799
total protein (g)	40	61	84
total carbohydrates (g)	253	385	530
total fat (g)	18	27	36
total saturated fat (g)	8	12	16
total cholesterol (mg)	31	46	61
total sodium (mg)	1730	2861	3460
total fiber (g)	10	16	21
% calories from fat	12	12	12

Light Rye Bread

This light rye bread has a slight rye flavor with the texture of white bread. A good starter rye bread that can be made in any machine.

1 lb	1½ lb	2 lb
5½ oz warm water	1 C warm water	11 oz warm water
1 T butter	1½ T butter	2 T butter
1 t salt	1½ t salt	2 t salt
1⅝ C bread flour	2⅜ C bread flour	3¼ C bread flour
5 T rye flour	½ C rye flour	⅝ C rye flour
1 T dry milk	1½ T dry milk	2 T dry milk
1½ t caraway seed, ground	2¼ t caraway seed, ground	1 T caraway seed, ground
2 T sugar	3 T sugar	¼ C sugar
¾ t active dry yeast	1¼ t active dry yeast	1½ t active dry yeast

Nutritional Analysis (per loaf, approximate)

Item	1 lb	1½ lb	2 lb
total calories (kcal)	1149	1705	2298
total protein (g)	33	49	66
total carbohydrates (g)	216	321	432
total fat (g)	16	24	33
total saturated fat (g)	8	12	16
total cholesterol (mg)	31	47	63
total sodium (mg)	2283	3425	4566
total fiber (g)	12	19	24
% calories from fat	13	13	13

Light Wheat Bread

This is a good basic wheat bread recipe to begin with. It uses enough bread flour to keep the texture similar to white bread, but adds the whole wheat flour for a richer wheat flavor.

1 lb	1½ lb	2 lb
5½ oz warm water	1 C warm water	11 oz warm water
1 T butter	1½ T butter	2 T butter
5 T whole wheat flour	½ C whole wheat flour	⅝ C whole wheat flour
1 t salt	1½ t salt	2 t salt
1½ C bread flour	2¼ C bread flour	3 C bread flour
1 T dry milk	1½ T dry milk	2 T dry milk
2 T sugar	3 T sugar	¼ C sugar
¾ t active dry yeast	1¼ t active dry yeast	1½ t active dry yeast

Nutritional Analysis (per loaf, approximate)

Item	1 lb	1½ lb	2 lb
total calories (kcal)	1090	1649	2180
total protein (g)	33	50	65
total carbohydrates (g)	205	310	409
total fat (g)	16	24	31
total saturated fat (g)	8	12	16
total cholesterol (mg)	31	47	63
total sodium (mg)	2283	3425	4566
total fiber (g)	10	16	21
% calories from fat	13	13	13

Oatmeal Bran Bread

There are four favorite grains in this smoothly textured bread, a flavorful treat that makes excellent sandwich bread.

1 lb	1½ lb	2 lb
⅔ C warm water	1C warm water	1⅓ C warm water
1½ T butter	2½ T butter	3 T butter
1 T molasses	1½ T molasses	2 T molasses
1½ T brown sugar	2½ T brown sugar	3 T brown sugar
½ t salt	½ t salt	1 t salt
2 T dry milk	3 T dry milk	¼ C dry milk
3 T rolled oats	¼ C rolled oats	⅜ C rolled oats
1 T bran	1½ T bran	2 T bran
½ C whole wheat flour	¾ C whole wheat flour	1 C whole wheat flour
1½ C bread flour	2¼ C bread flour	3 C bread flour
1½ t active dry yeast	2¼ t active dry yeast	1 T active dry yeast

Nutritional Analysis (per loaf, approximate)

Item	1 lb	1½ lb	2 lb
total calories (kcal)	1316	1998	2362
total protein (g)	41	62	83
total carbohydrates (g)	239	359	479
total fat (g)	23	37	46
total saturated fat (g)	12	19	23
total cholesterol (mg)	48	79	95
total sodium (mg)	1314	1468	2629
total fiber (g)	17	25	34
% calories from fat	16	16	16

Old-Fashioned Buttermilk Bread

This basic buttermilk bread is a basic white bread with a thicker texture resulting from the use of buttermilk as the liquid instead of water.

1 lb	1½ lb	2 lb
7 oz buttermilk	10 oz buttermilk	14 oz buttermilk
2 T honey	3 T honey	¼ C honey
1 T butter	1½ T butter	2 T butter
2 t wheat gluten	1½ T wheat gluten	1½ T wheat gluten
2 C bread flour	3 C bread flour	4 C bread flour
1 t salt	1½ t salt	2 t salt
1½ t active dry yeast	2¼ t active dry yeast	1 T active dry yeast

Nutritional Analysis (per loaf, approximate)

Item	1 lb	1½ lb	2 lb
total calories (kcal)	1356	2028	2722
total protein (g)	50	74	102
total carbohydrates (g)	246	368	492
total fat (g)	19	28	37
total saturated fat (g)	9	13	18
total cholesterol (mg)	38	56	75
total sodium (mg)	2480	3705	4963
total fiber (g)	3	4	6
% calories from fat	12	12	12

Onion–Caraway Bread

The fresh onion in this bread gives it a great aroma while baking.

1 lb	1½ lb	2 lb
⅔ C cottage cheese	1 C cottage cheese	1⅓ C cottage cheese
½ T butter	2 t butter	1 T butter
5 T warm water	½ C warm water	⅝ C warm water
2 t sugar	1 T sugar	1⅓ T sugar
¾ t salt	1½ t salt	1½ t salt
2 C bread flour	3 C bread flour	4 C bread flour
½ t baking soda	¾ t baking soda	1 t baking soda
2 T chopped onion	3 T chopped onion	¼ C chopped onion
2 t caraway seed	1 T caraway seed	1⅓ T caraway seed
1 t active dry yeast	1½ t active dry yeast	2 t active dry yeast

Nutritional Analysis (per loaf, approximate)

Item	1 lb	1½ lb	2 lb
total calories (kcal)	1241	1853	2482
total protein (g)	56	84	112
total carbohydrates (g)	218	327	436
total fat (g)	14	20	28
total saturated fat (g)	6	9	12
total cholesterol (mg)	28	39	56
total sodium (mg)	2909	5153	5818
total fiber (g)	10	15	20
% calories from fat	10	10	10

Onion & Cheese Bread

This zesty bread has a moist consistency with the tangy flavor of cheddar and onion. Excellent bread for toasting.

1 lb	1½ lb	2 lb
7 oz water	1¼ C water	14 oz water
1⅓ T powdered milk	2 T powdered milk	2⅔ T powdered milk
2 t sugar	1 T sugar	1⅓ T sugar
½ t salt	1 t salt	1 t salt
2⅛ C bread flour	3¼ C bread flour	4½ C bread flour
2 t dried onions	1 T dried onions	1⅓ T dried onions
3 T shredded sharp cheddar cheese	¼ C shredded sharp cheddar cheese	⅜ C shredded sharp cheddar cheese
½ t active dry yeast	1 t active dry yeast	1½ t active dry yeast

Nutritional Analysis (per loaf, approximate)

Item	1 lb	1½ lb	2 lb
total calories (kcal)	1257	1888	2596
total protein (g)	48	67	92
total carbohydrates (g)	231	347	478
total fat (g)	15	22	30
total saturated fat (g)	8	11	14
total cholesterol (mg)	33	49	65
total sodium (mg)	1251	1345	2502
total fiber (g)	2	3	4
% calories from fat	11	11	11

Onion–Mustard Bread

This is a tangy bread that is particularly good for sandwiches.

1 lb	1½ lb	2 lb
⅔ C milk	1 C milk	1⅓ C milk
2 t prepared mustard	1 T prepared mustard	1½ T prepared mustard
½ T olive oil	2½ t olive oil	1 T olive oil
1 egg	1 egg	2 eggs
½ T sugar	2¼ t sugar	1 T sugar
½ t salt	¾ t salt	1 t salt
2 C bread flour	3 C bread flour	4 C bread flour
¼ t black pepper	½ t black pepper	½ t black pepper
1 T minced onion	1½ T minced onion	2 T minced onion
1 t active dry yeast	1½ t active dry yeast	2 t active dry yeast

Nutritional Analysis (per loaf, approximate)

Item	1 lb	1½ lb	2 lb
total calories (kcal)	1259	1871	2518
total protein (g)	46	66	91
total carbohydrates (g)	216	325	432
total fat (g)	22	32	43
total saturated fat (g)	6	9	13
total cholesterol (mg)	203	214	406
total sodium (mg)	1369	2027	2738
total fiber (g)	8	12	17
% calories from fat	16	15	16

Poppy Seed Dilly Bread

"Dilly bread" is bread made with dill weed. This variation features plenty of interesting flavors with the addition of poppy seeds and onions.

1 lb	1½ lb	2 lb
⅔ C warm water	1 C warm water	1⅓ C warm water
1½ T butter	2 T butter	3 T butter
2 C bread flour	3 C bread flour	4 C bread flour
1½ T instant dry milk	2 T instant dry milk	3 T instant dry milk
1 T sugar	2 T sugar	2 T sugar
1½ T dried onions	2 T dried onions	3 T dried onions
1 t dill weed	1½ t dill weed	2 t dill weed
1 t poppy seeds	1½ t poppy seeds	2 t poppy seeds
½ t salt	1 t salt	1 t salt
1 t active dry yeast	1½ t active dry yeast	2 t active dry yeast

Nutritional Analysis (per loaf, approximate)

Item	1 lb	1½ lb	2 lb
total calories (kcal)	1261	1883	2521
total protein (g)	38	57	76
total carbohydrates (g)	222	338	444
total fat (g)	23	32	46
total saturated fat (g)	12	15	23
total cholesterol (mg)	47	63	94
total sodium (mg)	1290	2433	2579
total fiber (g)	3	5	7
% calories from fat	17	15	17

Prune Bread

This is white bread with a zip to it. The addition of orange peel and chopped prunes gives it a mild fruit flavor that tastes great toasted and buttered.

1 lb	1½ lb	2 lb
5 oz warm water	7½ oz warm water	10 oz warm water
1 T honey	1½ T honey	2 T honey
½ t salt	¾ t salt	1 t salt
1¾ C bread flour	2⅝ C bread flour	3½ C bread flour
½ t orange peel	¾ t orange peel	1 t orange peel
½ C prunes, chopped	¾ C prunes, chopped	1 C prunes, chopped
1½ t active dry yeast	2¼ t active dry yeast	1 T active dry yeast

Nutritional Analysis (per loaf, approximate)

Item	1 lb	1½ lb	2 lb
total calories (kcal)	1122	1684	2245
total protein (g)	33	50	66
total carbohydrates (g)	240	360	479
total fat (g)	5	7	9
total saturated fat (g)	1	1	1
total cholesterol (mg)	0	0	0
total sodium (mg)	1082	1623	2163
total fiber (g)	13	19	25
% calories from fat	4	4	4

Quick Onion Bread

This easy bread has a great texture and wonderful onion flavor enhanced by the applesauce and honey.

1 lb	1½ lb	2 lb
½ C water	¾ C water	1 C water
1 T applesauce	1½ T applesauce	2 T applesauce
1 T honey	1½ T honey	2 T honey
1 egg	1 egg	2 eggs
3 T dried onions	¼ C dried onions	⅜ C dried onions
2 C bread flour	3 C bread flour	4 C bread flour
¼ T powdered milk	¾ t powdered milk	1¼ t powdered milk
1 t salt	1½ t salt	2 t salt
1½ t active dry yeast	2 t active dry yeast	1 T active dry yeast

Nutritional Analysis (per loaf, approximate)

Item	1 lb	1½ lb	2 lb
total calories (kcal)	1205	1765	2410
total protein (g)	43	61	86
total carbohydrates (g)	232	347	463
total fat (g)	10	13	21
total saturated fat (g)	3 g	3	5
total cholesterol (mg)	214	214	428
total sodium (mg)	2216	3291	4432
total fiber (g)	4	6	8
% calories from fat	8	7	8

Seven Grain Honey Bread

Seven grain cereal typically contains cracked wheat, oats, rye barley, millet, flax and corn. A hearty breakfast cereal, it makes a wonderful bread. Until recent times, honey was the main sweetener used throughout the world, and it gives this bread a slightly sweet taste that complements the grains well. This recipe makes a smooth, even-textured bread.

1 lb	1½ lb	2 lb
⅓ C warm water	½ C warm water	⅔ C warm water
1½ T milk	2 T milk	3 T milk
1½ T honey	2½ T honey	3 T honey
1 T vegetable oil	1 T vegetable oil	2 T vegetable oil
1 T butter	1½ T butter	2 T butter
1 egg	1 egg	1 egg
⅓ C seven grain cereal, uncooked	½ C seven grain cereal, uncooked	⅔ C seven grain cereal, uncooked
½ t sugar	¾ t sugar	1 t sugar
1 t salt	1 t salt	2 t salt
1¾ C bread flour	2¾ C bread flour	3½ C bread flour
1 t active dry yeast	1½ t active dry yeast	2 t active dry yeast

Nutritional Analysis (per loaf, approximate)

Item	1 lb	1½ lb	2 lb
total calories (kcal)	1387	2065	2775
total protein (g)	40	59	80
total carbohydrates (g)	229	360	458
total fat (g)	35	43	70
total saturated fat (g)	11	15	22
total cholesterol (mg)	214	231	429
total sodium (mg)	2323	2391	4647
total fiber (g)	10	15	20
% calories from fat	23	19	23

Simple Oatmeal Bread

Although simple and quick, this bread still has the soft texture and traditionally sweet taste of oatmeal bread.

1 lb	1½ lb	2 lb
1 T butter	1½ T butter	2 T butter
½ C milk	¾ C milk	1 C milk
½ C warm water	¾ C warm water	1 C warm water
2⅓ C bread flour	3½ C bread flour	4½ C bread flour
2 T sugar	3 T sugar	¼ C sugar
1 t salt	1½ t salt	2 t salt
¼ C rolled oats	⅜ C rolled oats	½ C rolled oats
1 t active dry yeast	1½ t active dry yeast	2 t active dry yeast

Nutritional Analysis (per loaf, approximate)

Item	1 lb	1½ lb	2 lb
total calories (kcal)	1514	2273	2948
total protein (g)	47	71	92
total carbohydrates (g)	277	417	539
total fat (g)	22	33	44
total saturated fat (g)	11	16	21
total cholesterol (mg)	47	71	94
total sodium (mg)	2320	3480	4640
total fiber (g)	4	7	9
% calories from fat	13	13	14

Wheat–Corn Bread

The combination of wheat flour, white flour, and cornmeal make this bread a tasty variation of ordinary white bread, with a bit of crunchy texture.

1 lb	1½ lb	2 lb
3 T warm water	¼ C warm water	⅜ warm water
½ T honey	2½ t honey	1 T honey
1 egg	1 egg	2 egg
½ C milk	¾ C milk	1 C milk
1 T butter	2 T butter	2 T butter
½ t salt	¾ t salt	1 t salt
⅓ C white corn meal	½ C white corn meal	⅔ C white corn meal
3 T wheat germ	¼ C wheat germ	⅜ C wheat germ
½ C whole wheat flour	¾ C whole wheat flour	1 C whole wheat flour
1¼ C bread flour	1¾ C bread flour	2½ C bread flour
1 t active dry yeast	1½ t active dry yeast	2 t active dry yeast

Nutritional Analysis (per loaf, approximate)

Item	1 lb	1½ lb	2 lb
total calories (kcal)	1340	1961	2680
total protein (g)	48	67	96
total carbohydrates (g)	230	332	459
total fat (g)	26	43	53
total saturated fat (g)	12	21	24
total cholesterol (mg)	228	267	456
total sodium (mg)	1309	1993	2617
total fiber (g)	18	27	37
% calories from fat	18	19	18

Whole Wheat Bread

This is an excellent basic wheat bread; half of the flour is whole wheat. The wheat flavor and texture are rich; the white flour provides just enough texture to make the bread easy to slice and toast.

1 lb	1½ lb	2 lb
6 oz warm water	8 oz warm water	12 oz warm water
1 T butter	1½ T butter	2 T butter
1 t salt	1½ t salt	2 t salt
1 C bread flour	1½ C bread flour	2 C bread flour
1 C whole wheat flour	1½ C whole wheat flour	2 C whole wheat flour
1 T dry milk	1½ T dry milk	2 T dry milk
2 T sugar	3 T sugar	¼ C sugar
1 t active dry yeast	1½ t active dry yeast	2 t active dry yeast

Nutritional Analysis (per loaf, approximate)

Item	1 lb	1½ lb	2 lb
total calories (kcal)	1126	1688	2251
total protein (g)	36	54	72
total carbohydrates (g)	215	323	430
total fat (g)	16	24	32
total saturated fat (g)	8	12	16
total cholesterol (mg)	31	47	63
total sodium (mg)	2287	3429	4574
total fiber (g)	19	29	38
% calories from fat	13	13	13

FESTIVE BREADS

These breads are traditional on special occasions or holidays.

Alpine Easter Bread

A tangy white bread with the nutty flavor of almonds and the zest of lemon.

1 lb	1½ lb	2 lb
¼ C milk	⅜ C milk	½ C milk
4 T butter	½ C butter	½ C butter
1 oz warm water	1 oz warm water	2 oz warm water
1 egg	1 egg	2 eggs
½ t vanilla extract	¾ t vanilla extract	1 t vanilla extract
¼ t lemon extract	¼ t lemon extract	½ t lemon extract
¼ t sugar	½ t sugar	½ t sugar
2 C bread flour	3 C bread flour	4 C bread flour
½ t salt	½ t salt	1 t salt
1 t dried lemon peel	1½ t dried lemon peel	2 t dried lemon peel
1 T chopped almonds	1½ T chopped almonds	2 T chopped almonds
1 t active dry yeast	1½ t active dry yeast	2 t active dry yeast

Nutritional Analysis (per loaf, approximate)

Item	1 lb	1½ lb	2 lb
total calories (kcal)	1564	2516	3128
total protein (g)	44	64	88
total carbohydrates (g)	207	310	413
total fat (g)	61	112	122
total saturated fat (g)	32	62	64
total cholesterol (mg)	312	438	623
total sodium (mg)	1621	2103	3243
total fiber (g)	8	12	17
% calories from fat	36	40	36

Carrot Bread

A flavorful bread that is mildly sweet and excellent for toasting.

1 lb	1½ lb	2 lb
3 T vegetable oil	¼ C vegetable oil	⅜ C vegetable oil
1 egg	1 egg	2 eggs
3½ oz warm water	6 oz warm water	7 oz warm water
2½ T sugar	3½ T sugar	⅓ C sugar
½ t salt	¾ t salt	1 t salt
1¾ C bread flour	2½ C bread flour	3½ C bread flour
¼ t nutmeg	¼ t nutmeg	½ t nutmeg
¼ t cinnamon	½ t cinnamon	½ t cinnamon
½ C grated carrots	¾ C grated carrots	1 C grated carrots
¼ C raisins	⅜ C raisins	½ C raisins
1 t active dry yeast	1½ t active dry yeast	2 t active dry yeast

Nutritional Analysis (per loaf, approximate)

Item	1 lb	1½ lb	2 lb
total calories (kcal)	1557	2169	3130
total protein (g)	37	51	75
total carbohydrates (g)	242	347	487
total fat (g)	50	65	100
total saturated fat (g)	7	9	14
total cholesterol (mg)	181	181	361
total sodium (mg)	1151	1700	2302
total fiber (g)	10	15	20
% calories from fat	29	27	29

Cinnamon Cranberry Bread

If you like the tart, distinctive taste of cranberries, you'll love this bread. It is only lightly sweetened, so the original flavor of the cranberries is highlighted.

1 lb	1½ lb	2 lb
1 C water	1½ C water	2 C water
1 T vegetable oil	1½ T vegetable oil	2 T vegetable oil
1 t cinnamon	1½ t cinnamon	2 t cinnamon
1½ t salt	2 t salt	1 T salt
1 T dry milk	1½ T dry milk	2 T dry milk
1 T orange peel	1½ T orange peel	2 T orange peel
1 T sugar	1½ T sugar	2 T sugar
2¼ C bread flour	3¼ C bread flour	4½ C bread flour
1 t active dry yeast	1½ t active dry yeast	2 t active dry yeast

Add at mix cycle:

2½T fresh cranberries	¼ C fresh cranberries	½ C fresh cranberries

Nutritional Analysis (per loaf, approximate)

Item	1 lb	1½ lb	2 lb
total calories (kcal)	1345	1955	2690
total protein (g)	41	59	81
total carbohydrates (g)	244	354	488
total fat (g)	21	32	42
total saturated fat (g)	4	5	7
total cholesterol (mg)	8	12	15
total sodium (mg)	3243	4332	6487
total fiber (g)	4	5	7
% calories from fat	14	15	14

Cinnamon Swirl Orange Bread

This glazed bread is excellent for an after-dinner treat.

1 lb	1½ lb	2 lb
1½ T warm water	2½ T warm water	3 T warm water
¼ C milk	⅜ C milk	½ C milk
1 T margarine	1½ T margarine	2 T margarine
¼ C orange juice	⅜ C orange juice	½ C orange juice
1 egg	1 egg	2 eggs
2 T sugar	3 T sugar	¼ C sugar
½ t salt	¾ t salt	1 t salt
2 C bread flour	3 C bread flour	4 C bread flour
½ T cinnamon	2¼ t cinnamon	1 T cinnamon
1½ t active dry yeast	2¼ t active dry yeast	1 T active dry yeast
½ T grated orange peel	2¼ t grated orange peel	1 T grated orange peel

Nutritional Analysis (per loaf, approximate)

Item	1 lb	1½ lb	2 lb
total calories (kcal)	1343	1982	2685
total protein (g)	43	62	86
total carbohydrates (g)	239	359	479
total fat (g)	23	32	45
total saturated fat (g)	5	7	11
total cholesterol (mg)	189	193	378
total sodium (mg)	1293	1913	2587
total fiber (g)	10	16	21
% calories from fat	15	15	15

Festive Hawaiian Bread

For a different change of pace at your next party, try this festive bread.

1 lb	1½ lb	2 lb
2½ T milk	¼ C milk	⅓ C milk
3 T margarine	4 T margarine	⅜ C margarine
1 egg	1 egg	2 eggs
½ t coconut extract	1 t coconut extract	1 t coconut extract
¼ t salt	½ t salt	½ t salt
3½ T sugar	⅓ C sugar	½ C sugar
⅓ C potato flakes	½ C potato flakes	⅔ C potato flakes
2 C bread flour	3 C bread flour	4 C bread flour
1 t active dry yeast	1½ t active dry yeast	2 t active dry yeast

Nutritional Analysis (per loaf, approximate)

Item	1 lb	1½ lb	2 lb
total calories (kcal)	1626	2353	3253
total protein (g)	43	62	87
total carbohydrates (g)	259	389	518
total fat (g)	45	60	90
total saturated fat (g)	9	12	18
total cholesterol (mg)	218	221	435
total sodium (mg)	1038	1727	2075
total fiber (g)	3	5	6
% calories from fat	25	23	25

Honey–Mustard Bread

This is a great sandwich bread with a light wheat consistency and the distinctive flavor of honey and mustard.

1 lb	1½ lb	2 lb
½ C water	¾ C water	1 C water
2½ T honey	3½ T honey	⅓ C honey
¼ C chicken broth	⅜ C chicken broth	½ C chicken broth
5 t honey mustard	2½ T honey mustard	3⅓ T honey mustard
1½ C bread flour	2¼ C bread flour	3 C bread flour
½ C whole wheat flour	¾ C whole wheat flour	1 C whole wheat flour
2 t dry milk	1 T dry milk	1⅓ T dry milk
1 t chives, dried	1½ t chives, dried	2 t chives, dried
½ t salt	¾ t salt	1 t salt
½ t active dry yeast	1 t active dry yeast	4 t active dry yeast

Nutritional Analysis (per loaf, approximate)			
Item	1 lb	1½ lb	2 lb
total calories (kcal)	1183	1758	2367
total protein (g)	42	63	84
total carbohydrates (g)	243	360	486
total fat (g)	8	11	15
total saturated fat (g)	1	1	2
total cholesterol (mg)	1	2	2
total sodium (mg)	1830	2745	3660
total fiber (g)	10	16	21
% calories from fat	6	6	6

Jalapeño Cheese Bread

This flavorful bread is excellent with soup, salad, or any Mexican food. It's also a good breakfast bread.

1 lb	1½ lb	2 lb
6 oz water	9 oz water	1½ C water
½ t salt	1 t salt	1 t salt
4 t sugar	2 T sugar	3 T sugar
⅓ C Monterey Jack cheese	½ C Monterey Jack cheese	⅔ C Monterey Jack cheese
2½ T chopped jalapeño	4 T chopped jalapeño	3⅓ T chopped jalapeño
2 C bread flour	3 C bread flour	4 C bread flour
1 t active dry yeast	1½ t active dry yeast	2 t active dry yeast

Nutritional Analysis

Item	1 lb	1½ lb	2 lb
total calories (kcal)	1219	1817	2438
total protein (g)	44	66	88
total carbohydrates (g)	221	328	442
total fat (g)	16	24	32
total saturated fat (g)	8	12	16
total cholesterol (g)	33	50	66
total sodium (mg)	1280	1920	2560
total fiber (g)	2	4	5
% calories from fat	12	12	12

Multigrain Garlic–Dill Bread

This is a flavorful variation on a basic bread. The garlic, dill weed, and yogurt add a particular zest to the loaf.

1 lb	1½ lb	2 lb
½ C warm water	¾ C warm water	1 C warn water
⅓ C plain yogurt	½ C plain yogurt	⅔ C plain yogurt
1 T olive oil	1½ T olive oil	2 T olive oil
¼ C rolled oats	⅜ C rolled oats	½ C rolled oats
¼ C cracked wheat	⅜ C cracked wheat	½ C cracked wheat
1½ t brown sugar	2¼ t brown sugar	1 T brown sugar
¾ t salt	1¼ t salt	1½ t salt
1¾ C bread flour	2¾ C bread flour	3½ C bread flour
1½ t minced garlic	2¼ t minced garlic	1 T minced garlic
1 t dill weed	1½ t dill weed	2 t dill weed
1 t active dry yeast	1 t active dry yeast	2 t active dry yeast

Nutritional Analysis (per loaf, approximate)

Item	1 lb	1½ lb	2 lb
total calories (kcal)	1146	1781	2293
total protein (g)	37	57	73
total carbohydrates (g)	199	311	398
total fat (g)	22	33	43
total saturated fat (g)	4	6	9
total cholesterol (mg)	10	14	19
total sodium (mg)	1650	2741	3299
total fiber (g)	9	14	18
% calories from fat	17	17	17

Peanut Butter Bread

The peanut butter in this bread gives it a smooth texture. It is excellent for toasting.

1 lb	1½ lb	2 lb
1 egg	1 egg	2 eggs
6 oz milk	9 oz milk	12 oz milk
2 C bread flour	3 C bread flour	4 C bread flour
½ t salt	¾ t salt	1 t salt
½ C sugar	¾ C sugar	1 C sugar
¾ C peanut butter	1⅛ C peanut butter	1½ C peanut butter
1 t active dry yeast	1½ t active dry yeast	2 t active dry yeast

Nutritional Analysis (per loaf, approximate)

Item	1 lb	1½ lb	2 lb
total calories (kcal)	2694	4009	5387
total protein (g)	93	137	186
total carbohydrates (g)	349	523	697
total fat (g)	111	165	223
total saturated fat (g)	24	36	48
total cholesterol (mg)	204	215	408
total sodium (mg)	2136	3177	4272
total fiber (g)	19	29	38
% calories from fat	36	36	36

Poppy Seed Loaf

A great party bread that is especially good on the table with other finger foods.

Make poppy seed dip for the bread by combining 4 tablespoons of melted butter and ¼ cup poppy seeds. Get the bread from the bread machine while warm, tear or cut pieces from the loaf, and dip.

1 lb	1½ lb	2 lb
½ C warm water	¾ C warm water	1 C warm water
¼ C milk	⅜ C milk	½ C milk
½ T shortening	2 t shortening	1 T shortening
½ t salt	¾ t salt	1 t salt
1 T sugar	1½ T sugar	2 T sugar
2 C bread flour	3 C bread flour	4 C bread flour
½ T poppy seeds	2¼ t poppy seeds	1 T poppy seeds
1 t active dry yeast	1½ t active dry yeast	2 t active dry yeast

Nutritional Analysis (per loaf, approximate)

Item	1 lb	1½ lb	2 lb
total calories (kcal)	1167	1741	2334
total protein (g)	37	56	74
total carbohydrates (g)	217	325	433
total fat (g)	15	22	30
total saturated fat (g)	4	5	8
total cholesterol (mg)	8	12	17
total sodium (mg)	1108	1662	2216
total fiber (g)	9	14	18
% calories from fat	12	11	12

Poppy Seed Prune Bread

A fun bread to serve at parties and get-togethers.

1 lb	1½ lb	2 lb
¼ C warm water	⅜ C warm water	½ C warm water
¼ C milk	⅜ C milk	½ C milk
1 T butter	2 T butter	2 T butter
1 egg	1 egg	2 eggs
2 t brown sugar	1 T brown sugar	1⅓ T brown sugar
¾ t salt	1¼ t salt	1½ t salt
1¾ C bread flour	2⅝ C bread flour	3½ C bread flour
1½ T poppy seeds	2¼ T poppy seeds	3 T poppy seeds
½ C prunes, chopped	¾ C prunes, chopped	1 C prunes, chopped
¼ t lemon peel	½ t lemon peel	½ t lemon peel
1 t active dry yeast	1½ t active dry yeast	2 t active dry yeast

Nutritional Analysis (per loaf, approximate)

Item	1 lb	1½ lb	2 lb
total calories (kcal)	1346	2038	2693
total protein (g)	42	60	84
total carbohydrates (g)	234	350	467
total fat (g)	28	46	56
total saturated fat (g)	11	19	22
total cholesterol (mg)	220	254	439
total sodium (mg)	1815	3019	3629
total fiber (g)	16	24	32
% calories from fat	19	20	19

Soft Cheese Bread

This bread has the soft, spongy texture of oatmeal bread with the pizzazz of tangy cheese.

1 lb	1½ lb	2 lb
½ C water	¾ C water	1 C water
⅔ C shredded sharp cheddar cheese	1 C shredded sharp cheddar cheese	1⅓ C shredded sharp cheddar cheese
1 egg	1 egg	2 eggs
2 t olive oil	1 T olive oil	1⅓ T olive oil
1⅔ C bread flour	2½ C bread flour	3½ C bread flour
⅔ C rolled oats	1 C rolled oats	1⅓ C rolled oats
2⅔ T powdered milk	¼ C powdered milk	⅓ C powdered milk
1 t salt	1½ t salt	2 t salt
2 t sugar	1 T sugar	1⅓ T sugar
1 t active dry yeast	1½ t active dry yeast	2 t active dry yeast

Nutritional Analysis (per loaf, approximate)

Item	1 lb	1½ lb	2 lb
total calories (kcal)	1640	2422	3362
total protein (g)	68	99	139
total carbohydrates (g)	221	332	459
total fat (g)	52	76	105
total saturated fat (g)	24	34	47
total cholesterol (mg)	313	363	625
total sodium (mg)	2755	4103	5511
total fiber (g)	7	12	15
% calories from fat	29	28	28

Sweet Potato Wheat Twist

A soft-textured bread with a distinctive sweet potato flavor. Excellent with soup.

1 lb	1½ lb	2 lb
2½ T warm water	3¾ T warm water	⅓ C warm water
⅓ C yams	½ C yams	⅔ C yams
¼ C buttermilk	⅜ C buttermilk	½ C buttermilk
½ T butter	1 T butter	1 T butter
½ T honey	2½ t honey	1 T honey
1 egg	1 egg	2 eggs
½ t salt	¾ t salt	1 t salt
1¾ C bread flour	2⅝ C bread flour	3½ C bread flour
½ C whole wheat flour	¾ C whole wheat flour	1 C whole wheat flour
1½ t active dry yeast	2¼ t active dry yeast	1 T active dry yeast

Nutritional Analysis (per loaf, approximate)

Item	1 lb	1½ lb	2 lb
total calories (kcal)	1308	1961	2616
total protein (g)	47	68	95
total carbohydrates (g)	244	367	488
total fat (g)	16	25	32
total saturated fat (g)	6	10	12
total cholesterol (mg)	198	215	396
total sodium (mg)	1258	1889	2516
total fiber (g)	17	25	33
% calories from fat	11	11	11

Three Kings Bread

Called *Rosca de los Reyes* in Latin America, this bread is customarily baked to celebrate Twelfth Night (January 6th). In its normal form, the bread is baked in a ring shape and garnished with nuts and candied fruits. Often, a tiny doll or an uncooked lima bean is hidden in the bread. The person receiving the bean or doll hosts a party on February 2nd, *El dia de la candelaria.*

1 lb	1½ lb	2 lb
⅓ C warm water	½ C warm water	⅔ C warm water
4 T butter	½ C butter	½ C butter
1 egg	1 egg	2 eggs
1¾ C bread flour	2⅝ C bread flour	3½ C bread flour
1½ T dry milk	2½ T dry milk	3 T dry milk
2 T sugar	3 T sugar	¼ C sugar
½ t salt	¾ t salt	1 t salt
2½ T raisins	3½ T raisins	⅓ C raisins
2½ T walnuts, chopped	4 T walnuts, chopped	⅓ C walnuts, chopped
1 T candied cherries, chopped	1½ T candied cherries, chopped	2 T candied cherries, chopped
1 t grated orange peel	1½ t grated orange peel	2 t grated orange peel
1 t grated lemon rind	1½ t grated lemon rind	2 t grated lemon rind
1½ t active dry yeast	2¼ t active dry yeast	1 T active dry yeast

(Nutritional analysis is on next page).

Three Kings Bread Nutritional Analysis (per loaf, approximate)

Item	1 lb	1½ lb	2 lb
total calories (kcal)	1582	2542	3177
total protein (g)	41	60	82
total carbohydrates (g)	229	342	461
total fat (g)	57	106	114
total saturated fat (g)	31	59	61
total cholesterol (mg)	304	428	609
total sodium (mg)	1638	2667	3277
total fiber (g)	9	13	18
% calories from fat	32	37	32

Tomato Rye Bread

This unique bread combines the distinct flavor of rye and caraway with the tangy vegetable juice for a wonderful bread that is great with salads.

1 lb	1½ lb	2 lb
¼ C chopped tomoato	⅜ C chopped tomato	½ C chopped tomato
1 T olive oil	1½ T olive oil	2 T olive oil
7 oz V8 vegetable juice	10 oz V8 vegetable juice	14 oz V8 vegetable juice
1¾C bread flour	2¾C bread flour	3½ C bread flour
½ C rye flour	¾ C rye flour	1 C rye flour
1 T sugar	1½ T sugar	2 T sugar
1 t salt	1½ t salt	2 t salt
1 T caraway seed	1½ T caraway seed	2 T caraway seed
1 t active dry yeast	1½ t active dry yeast	2 t active dry yeast

Nutritional Analysis (per loaf, approximate)

Item	1 lb	1½ lb	2 lb
total calories (kcal)	1295	2002	2590
total protein (g)	38	59	76
total carbohydrates (g)	242	375	484
total fat (g)	20	30	40
total saturated fat (g)	3	4	5
total cholesterol (mg)	0	0	0
total sodium (mg)	2869	4251	5737
total fiber (g)	6	9	12
% calories from fat	14	14	14

Wild Rice Bread

Wild rice is difficult to find growing wild, and hence fairly expensive. This recipe is made even better if you can use wild rice flour instead of the regular white rice flour called for. If you have a grinder or food processor that can process grains into flour, you can simply make your own wild rice flour. Otherwise, use the commercially available rice flour and use the cooked wild rice to give the bread the wild rice flavor. Be sure to drain the cooked rice well and let it dry or a while before using it in the recipe. The cooked wild rice is included as a dry ingredient in the ratio, so you don't want wet rice or your bread will not rise properly.

1 lb	1½ lb	2 lb
¾ C warm water	9 oz warm water	1½ C warm water
1½ T vegetable oil	2½ T vegetable oil	3 T vegetable oil
¼ C rice flour	⅜ C rice flour	½ C rice flour
½ t salt	¾ t salt	1 t salt
1½ C bread flour	2½ C bread flour	3 C bread flour
⅓ C cooked wild rice	½ C cooked wild rice	⅔ C cooked wild rice
1 t active dry yeast	1½ t active dry yeast	2 t active dry yeast

Nutritional Analysis (per loaf, approximate)

Item	1 lb	1½ lb	2 lb
total calories (kcal)	1134	1855	2268
total protein (g)	31	50	61
total carbohydrates (g)	194	316	388
total fat (g)	25	41	50
total saturated fat (g)	3	5	6
total cholesterol (mg)	0	0	0
total sodium (mg)	1079	1619	2158
total fiber (g)	8	13	16
% calories from fat	20	20	20

INTERNATIONAL BREADS

These breads have their origins all around the world. Many are traditional loaves of their respective countries, modified for baking in the bread machine.

Armenian Sesame Bread

A hearty and rich white bread, perfect for sandwiches.

1 lb	1½ lb	2 lb
2 T warm water	3 T warm water	¼ C warm water
½ C milk	¾ C milk	1 C milk
1 T olive oil	1½ T olive oil	2 T olive oil
½ T butter	2½ t butter	1 T butter
2½ t sugar	1½ T sugar	1⅔ T sugar
¾ t salt	1 t salt	1½ t salt
2 C bread flour	3 C bread flour	4 C bread flour
1½ T sesame seeds	2⅓ T sesame seeds	3 T sesame seeds
1 t active dry yeast	1½ t active dry yeast	2 t active dry yeast

Nutritional Analysis (per loaf, approximate)

Item	1 lb	1½ lb	2 lb
total calories (kcal)	1368	2078	2737
total protein (g)	42	63	84
total carbohydrates (g)	218	330	435
total fat (g)	36	55	71
total saturated fat (g)	10	15	19
total cholesterol (mg)	32	50	64
total sodium (mg)	1731	2339	3461
total fiber (g)	8	12	15
% calories from fat	24	24	24

Broa: Portuguese Corn Bread

In Portugal, this bread frequently is served with caldo verde, a type of bean soup. It was brought to the United States by the descendants of Portuguese fishermen from the Azores. The bread goes well with almost any soup or salad, and is delicious by itself with butter and jam or jelly.

1 lb	1½ lb	2 lb
1 C boiling water	1½ C boiling water	2 C boiling water
1 T olive oil	1½ T olive oil	2 T olive oil
½ t sugar	¾ t sugar	1 t sugar
½ C yellow corn flour, whole grain	¾ C yellow corn flour, whole grain	1 C yellow corn flour, whole grain
½ t salt	¾ t salt	1 t salt
1½ C bread flour	2¼ C bread flour	3 C bread flour
1½ t active dry yeast	2¼ t active dry yeast	1 T active dry yeast

Nutritional Analysis (per loaf, approximate)

Item	1 lb	1½ lb	2 lb
total calories (kcal)	1098	1647	2196
total protein (g)	31	47	62
total carbohydrates (g)	198	298	397
total fat (g)	19	29	39
total saturated fat (g)	3	4	5
total cholesterol (mg)	0	0	0
total sodium (mg)	1083	1625	2166
total fiber (g)	14	22	29
% calories from fat	16	16	16

Chive and Garlic Bread

This is a zippy variation of white bread that is fantastic with pasta or soups. Saute the garlic in butter for 1–2 minutes; then let cool before adding to the mixture.

1 lb	1½ lb	2 lb
2 t butter	1 T butter	1½ T butter
7 oz milk	1¼ C milk	14 oz milk
3 cloves garlic	5 cloves garlic	6 cloves garlic
2 C bread flour	3 C bread flour	4 C bread flour
3½ T grated parmesan cheese	⅓ C grated parmesan cheese	½ C grated parmesan cheese
1½ T chopped fresh chives	2 T chopped fresh chives	3 T chopped fresh chives
2 t sugar	1 T sugar	1½ T sugar
½ t salt	¾ t salt	1 t salt
½ t active dry yeast	1 t active dry yeast	2 t active dry yeast

Nutritional Analysis (per loaf, approximate)

Item	1 lb	1½ lb	2 lb
total calories (kcal)	1332	2007	2700
total protein (g)	50	76	102
total carbohydrates (g)	221	333	446
total fat (g)	26	39	53
total saturated fat (g)	14	21	29
total cholesterol (mg)	65	98	135
total sodium (mg)	1661	2496	3344
total fiber (g)	2	3	5
% calories from fat	18	18	18

Crescia al Formaggio

Crescia is a conjugated form of the Italian verb *crescere,* which means "to grow." This bread, rich in cheese flavor, rises steadily. The cheese in the bread is best melted in the microwave ahead of time so that it adds to the liquidity of the bread during mixing. When the bread is not baked in the bread machine, the cheese is typically folded into the dough before the final rise and bake. Using the bread machine can work too, but as the cheese melts, it adds to the liquidity of the bread, which can cause the loaf to fall from a high rise. That's why it is better to melt the cheese before adding it to the machine.

1 lb	1½ lb	2 lb
7 oz warm water	1¼ C warm water	14 oz warm water
4 T butter	⅜ C butter	½ C butter
⅓ C Swiss cheese, shredded & melted	½ C Swiss cheese, shredded & melted	⅔ C Swiss cheese, shredded & melted
¼ t sugar	½ t sugar	½ t sugar
¼ t salt	½ t salt	½ t salt
⅓ C grated parmesan cheese	½ C grated parmesan cheese	⅔ C grated parmesan cheese
1¾ C bread flour	2¾ C bread flour	3½ C bread flour
1½ t active dry yeast	2¼ t active dry yeast	1 T active dry yeast

Nutritional Analysis (per loaf, approximate)

Item	1 lb	1½ lb	2 lb
total calories (kcal)	1552	2392	3104
total protein (g)	53	82	107
total carbohydrates (g)	180	282	359
total fat (g)	68	102	136
total saturated fat (g)	41	61	81
total cholesterol (mg)	178	267	357
total sodium (mg)	1604	2673	3208
total fiber (g)	7	12	15
% calories from fat	40	39	40

Feta–Garlic Bread

A traditional Greek bread that goes well with salad.

1 lb	1½ lb	2 lb
¾ C warm water	9 oz warm water	1½ C warm water
1½ t sugar	2¼ t sugar	1 T sugar
1½ t salt	2¼ t salt	1 T salt
2⅛ C bread flour	3¼ C bread flour	4½ C bread flour
1 T garlic, chopped	1½ T garlic, chopped	2 T garlic, chopped
¼ t ground pepper	¼ t ground pepper	½ t ground pepper
¼ C feta cheese	⅜ C feta cheese	½ C feta cheese
1 t active dry yeast	1½ t active dry yeast	2 t active dry yeast

Nutritional Analysis (per loaf, approximate)

Item	1 lb	1½ lb	2 lb
total calories (kcal)	1175	1792	2473
total protein (g)	41	63	86
total carbohydrates (g)	223	341	471
total fat (g)	11	17	23
total saturated fat (g)	5	8	10
total cholesterol (mg)	25	38	50
total sodium (mg)	3529	5293	7058
total fiber (g)	8	13	18
% calories from fat	9	9	8

Haidd: Welsh Barley Bread

Barley is a staple grain in many parts of the world. Making a loaf out of pure barley flour is difficult in the bread machine, since barley doesn't have the same rising characteristics as wheat flour. Although the authetic bread would be 100% barley flour, we have inserted some bread flour in the recipe to make it work better in the bread machine. The extra yeast (more than normal for the bread machine) is necessary because of the reduced rising capacity of the barley flour.

This bread is a favorite in Wales. Similar breads are found in Ireland, Scotland, Egypt, and many other parts of the world. If you want the authentic bread, substitute barley flour for the bread flour called for here, and use the dough setting on your machine. Remove the dough from the machine at the end of the cycle and bake the bread in a 400°F (204.4°C) oven for 25 minutes. It is best eaten hot with butter and honey.

1 lb	1½ lb	2 lb
7 oz warm water	11 oz warm water	14 oz warm water
2 t butter	1 T butter	1⅓ T butter
½ t sugar	¾ t sugar	1 t sugar
1⅔ C barley flour	2½ C barley flour	3⅓ C barley flour
½ t salt	¾ t salt	1 t salt
½ C bread flour	¾ C bread flour	1 C bread flour
2 t active dry yeast	1 T active dry yeast	1⅓ T active dry yeast
4 t gluten	2 T gluten	2⅔ T gluten

(Nutritional analysis is on next page).

Haidd Nutritional Analysis (per loaf, approximate)

Item	1 lb	1½ lb	2 lb
total calories (kcal)	1432	2147	2863
total protein (g)	50	75	99
total carbohydrates (g)	280	420	560
total fat (g)	16	24	32
total saturated fat (g)	6	10	13
total cholesterol (mg)	20	31	41
total sodium (mg)	1191	1787	2382
total fiber (g)	57	85	114
% calories from fat	10	10	10

Italian Herb Bread

This bread is great with any Italian dish or any salad. It's also good for making salad croutons.

1 lb	1½ lb	2 lbs
¾ C water	9 oz water	1½ C water
2 T applesauce	3 T applesauce	¼ C applesauce
1 T honey	1½ T honey	2 T honey
2 C whole wheat flour	3 C whole wheat flour	4 C whole wheat flour
1½ T wheat gluten	2¼ T wheat gluten	3 T wheat gluten
2 T dried onions	3 T dried onions	¼ C dried onions
2 t chives, freeze dried	1 T chives, freeze dried	1⅓ T chives, freeze dried
1 t salt	1½ t salt	2 t salt
¾ t garlic powder	1 t garlic powder	1½ t garlic powder
¾ t oregano	1¼ t oregano	1½ t oregano
¼ t basil	¼ t basil	½ t basil
1½ t active dry yeast	2¼ t active dry yeast	1 T active dry yeast

Nutritional Analysis (per loaf, approximate)

Item	1 lb	1½ lb	2 lb
total calories (kcal)	1048	1571	2095
total protein (g)	54	81	109
total carbohydrates (g)	210	314	420
total fat (g)	7	10	13
total saturated fat (g)	1	2	2
total cholesterol (mg)	0	0	0
total sodium (mg)	2188	2181	4375
total fiber (g)	32	49	65
% calories from fat	5	5	5

Italian Pork Bread

The Italians have a great tradition of combining meat with their bread, as in pizza, calzones, and the like. This bread has a great flavor and is best eaten right out of the bread machine while still hot. Because the bread contains fresh pork, it is best to bake only as much as you plan to eat while it is hot and freshly baked.

1 lb	1½ lb	2 lb
5 oz warm water	7½ oz warm water	10 oz warm water
1½ T sugar	2¼ T sugar	3 T sugar
1¾ C bread flour	2⅝ C bread flour	3½ C bread flour
½ t salt	¾ t salt	1 t salt
¼ t black pepper	⅜ t black pepper	½ t black pepper
½ C pork roast, cooked & shredded	¾ C pork roast, cooked & shredded	1 C pork roast, cooked & shredded
1 t active dry yeast	1½ t active dry yeast	2 t active dry yeast

Nutritional Analysis (per loaf, approximate)

Item	1 lb	1½ lb	2 lb
total calories (kcal)	1311	1966	2622
total protein (g)	57	85	114
total carbohydrates (g)	195	292	389
total fat (g)	32	47	63
total saturated fat (g)	11	16	21
total cholesterol (mg)	101	152	203
total sodium (mg)	1410	2116	2821
total fiber (g)	7	11	14
% calories from fat	22	22	22

Lithuanian Potato Bread

Using fresh potato enhances the flavor of this variation of the perennial favorite, potato bread. Note the variety of liquids used here: water, milk, butter, sour cream, and egg.

1 lb	1½ lb	2 lb
1½ T warm water	2½ T warm water	3 T warm water
3 oz milk	4½ oz milk	6 oz milk
1 egg	1 egg	2 eggs
1 T sour cream	1½ T sour cream	2 T sour cream
½ T butter	2½ t butter	1 T butter
¼ t sugar	⅜ t sugar	½ t sugar
2¼ C bread flour	3¼ C bread flour	4½ C bread flour
1 t salt	1½ t salt	2 t salt
¼ C potato, grated	⅜ C potato, grated	½ C potato, grated
1 t active dry yeast	1½ t active dry yeast	2 t active dry yeast

Nutritional Analysis (per loaf, approximate)

Item	1 lb	1½ lb	2 lb
total calories (kcal)	1336	1919	2673
total protein (g)	47	66	95
total carbohydrates (g)	234	338	468
total fat (g)	21	30	42
total saturated fat (g)	9	14	19
total cholesterol (mg)	214	233	428
total sodium (mg)	2302	3436	4604
total fiber (g)	9	13	18
% calories from fat	14	14	14

Olive, Mint, and Onion Bread

This unusual bread originated in Cyprus, where olive trees abound, and stems from the traditional Greek bread called *eliopsomo*.

1 lb	1½ lb	2 lb
5½ oz warm water	8½ oz warm water	11 oz warm water
1 T olive oil	1½ T olive oil	2 T olive oil
¼ t sugar	½ t sugar	½ t sugar
¼ C whole wheat flour	⅜ C whole wheat flour	½ C whole wheat flour
1½ C bread flour	2¼ C bread flour	3 C bread flour
½ t salt	¾ t salt	1 t salt
1 t dried mint flakes	1½ t dried mint flakes	2 t dried mint flakes
4 T onions, chopped	⅜ C onions, chopped	½ C onions, chopped
2 T black olives, chopped	3 T black olives, chopped	¼ C black olives, chopped
1 t active dry yeast	1½ t active dry yeast	2 t active dry yeast

Nutritional Analysis (per loaf, approximate)

Item	1 lb	1½ lb	2 lb
total calories (kcal)	1006	1511	2012
total protein (g)	31	46	62
total carbohydrates (g)	176	265	352
total fat (g)	20	29	39
total saturated fat (g)	3	4	5
total cholesterol (mg)	0	0	0
total sodium (mg)	1374	2061	2747
total fiber (g)	10	15	20
% calories from fat	18	18	18

Parmesan Bread

This is a wonderful Italian flavored bread that is great with pasta of all kinds, or toasted as garlic bread.

1 lb	1½ lb	2 lb
1 C water	1½ C water	2 C water
2½ T olive oil	3½ T olive oil	⅓ C olive oil
3 t honey	1½ T honey	2 T honey
1½ t salt	2 t salt	1 T salt
2 t garlic powder	1 T garlic powder	1⅓ T garlic powder
2⅓ C bread flour	3½ C bread flour	4½ C bread flour
⅔ C grated parmesan cheese	1 C grated parmesan cheese	1⅓ C grated parmesan cheese
2½ T dry milk	3½ T dry milk	⅓ C nonfat dry milk
½ t active dry yeast	1 t active dry yeast	1 t active dry yeast

Nutritional Analysis (per loaf, approximate)

Item	1 lb	1½ lb	2 lb
total calories (kcal)	1915	2840	3749
total protein (g)	75	86	147
total carbohydrates (g)	267	399	516
total fat (g)	60	86	119
total saturated fat (g)	18	27	36
total cholesterol (mg)	57	85	113
total sodium (mg)	4566	6306	9131
total fiber (g)	2	2	4
% calories from fat	28	27	29

Turmeric and Caraway Bread

This African-style bread can be made more authentic by substituting red palm oil for the olive oil. If red palm oil is not available, try mixing corn oil with a pinch of paprika.

1 lb	1½ lb	2 lb
6 oz warm water	9 oz warm water	12 oz warm water
1 T honey	1½ T honey	2 T honey
1 T olive oil	1½ T olive oil	2 T olive oil
½ T turmeric	2¼ t turmeric	1 T turmeric
½ t salt	¾ t salt	1 t salt
2 C bread flour	3 C bread flour	4 C bread flour
1¼ t caraway seed	2 t caraway seed	2½ t caraway seed
1½ t active dry yeast	2¼ t active dry yeast	1 T active dry yeast

Nutritional Analysis (per loaf, approximate)

Item	1 lb	1½ lb	2 lb
total calories (kcal)	1212	1819	2424
total protein (g)	36	54	72
total carbohydrates (g)	222	333	444
total fat (g)	19	29	38
total saturated fat (g)	3	4	5
total cholesterol (mg)	0	0	0
total sodium (mg)	1082	1623	2164
total fiber (g)	10	15	20
% calories from fat	14	14	14

Yemarina Yewotet Dabo Bread
(Ethiopian Honey Bread)

The unique flavor of this bread comes from the interesting combination of spices.

1 lb	1½ lb	2 lb
1½ T warm water	2¼ T warm water	3 T warm water
1 egg	1 egg	2 eggs
3 T honey	¼ C honey	⅜ C honey
¼ C milk	½ C milk	½ C milk
2½ T butter	3½ T butter	⅓ C butter
½ T ground coriander	2¼ t ground coriander	1 T ground coriander
¼ t ground cinnamon	½ t ground cinnamon	½ t ground cinnamon
⅛ t ground cloves	2 dashes ground cloves	¼ t ground cloves
½ t salt	¾ t salt	1 t salt
2 C bread flour	3 C bread flour	4 C bread flour
1½ t active dry yeast	2¼ t active dry yeast	1 T active dry yeast

Nutritional Analysis (per loaf, approximate)

Item	1 lb	1½ lb	2 lb
total calories (kcal)	1554	2262	3142
total protein (g)	43	63	86
total carbohydrates (g)	257	379	515
total fat (g)	40	56	83
total saturated fat (g)	21	30	44
total cholesterol (mg)	266	305	541
total sodium (mg)	1451	2136	2941
total fiber (g)	9	13	18
% calories from fat	23	22	24

TRADITIONAL BREADS

These breads have their roots in the American past and are traditional favorites in various parts of the United States.

Bacon–Cheese Bread

A wonderful variation on white bread that has a moist texture and is great for sandwiches. You can use bacon or cheese substitutes in lieu of the real thing. The nutritional analysis doesn't include the cheese or bacon, since that varies according to the type you use.

1 lb	1½ lb	2 lb
⅔ C milk	1 C milk	1⅓ C milk
1 T butter	1⅓ T butter	2 T butter
2 t sugar	1 T sugar	1⅓ T sugar
½ t salt	½ t salt	1 t salt
2 C bread flour	3 C bread flour	4 C bread flour
1 t active dry yeast	1½ t active dry yeast	2 t active dry yeast

At the mix cycle add:

¼ C shredded cheddar cheese	6 T shredded cheddar cheese	½ C shredded cheddar cheese
¼ C cooked, crumbled bacon	6 T cooked, crumbled bacon	½ C cooked, crumbled bacon

Nutritional Analysis (per loaf, approximate)

Item	1 lb	1½ lb	2 lb
total calories (kcal)	1233	1834	2467
total protein (g)	40	60	80
total carbohydrates (g)	216	324	432
total fat (g)	22	30	43
total saturated fat (g)	11	16	22
total cholesterol (mg)	53	74	106
total sodium (mg)	1269	1351	2538
total fiber (g)	2	3	4
% calories from fat	16	15	16

Blue Ribbon Potato Bread

Here is a simple loaf of potato bread that has very few ingredients to round up, is quick to put together, and is very tasty.

1 lb	1½ lb	2 lb
⅔ C warm water	1 C warm water	1⅓ C warm water
1 t salt	1½ t salt	2 t salt
2½ t butter	1½ T butter	1⅔ T butter
5 t potato flakes	2½ T potato flakes	3⅓ T potato flakes
1 T sugar	1½ T sugar	2 T sugar
2 C bread flour	3 C bread flour	4 C bread flour
1 t active dry yeast	1½ t active dry yeast	2 t active dry yeast

Nutritional Analysis (per loaf, approximate)

Item	1 lb	1½ lb	2 lb
total calories (kcal)	1150	1749	2299
total protein (g)	35	52	70
total carbohydrates (g)	217	325	433
total fat (g)	14	24	28
total saturated fat (g)	7	12	13
total cholesterol (mg)	26	46	51
total sodium (mg)	2245	3397	4491
total fiber (g)	8	12	16
% calories from fat	11	13	11

Blue Ribbon Rye Bread

An excellent basic light rye bread.

1 lb	1½ lb	2 lb
3 T molasses	¼ C molasses	⅜ C molasses
1½ T butter	2½ T butter	3 T butter
½ C warm water	¾ C warm water	1 C warm water
1 egg	1 egg	2 eggs
½ C rye flour	¾ C rye flour	1 C rye flour
½ t salt	¾ t salt	1 t salt
2 C bread flour	3 C bread flour	4 C bread flour
1 t active dry yeast	1½ t active dry yeast	2 t active dry yeast
1 t caraway seed	1½ t caraway seed	2 t caraway seed

Nutritional Analysis (per loaf, approximate)			
Item	1 lb	1½ lb	2 lb
total calories (kcal)	1566	2316	3133
total protein (g)	45	65	90
total carbohydrates (g)	284	418	568
total fat (g)	27	42	55
total saturated fat (g)	13	20	26
total cholesterol (mg)	227	257	453
total sodium (mg)	1329	1991	2657
total fiber (g)	16	24	32
% calories from fat	16	16	16

Buha (Adobe Bread)

This is a simple bread, characteristic of the Southwest. The Pueblo Indians call this bread *buha*. It is generally baked on feast days in batches of up to 120 loaves. It gets the nickname "adobe bread" because it is baked in large adobe ovens, heated by wood fires. Of course your bread machine is not going to yield the wood-smoked flavor of those ovens, but you can come close to the chewy texture with this recipe.

1 lb	1½ lb	2 lb
⅔ C warm water	1 C warm water	1⅓ C warm water
1½ T cooking oil	2¼ T cooking oil	3 T cooking oil
½ t salt	¾ t salt	1 t salt
2 C bread flour	3 C bread flour	4 C bread flour
1 t active dry yeast	1½ t active dry yeast	2 t active dry yeast

Nutritional Analysis (per loaf, approximate)

Item	1 lb	1½ lb	2 lb
total calories (kcal)	1182	1772	2363
total protein (g)	34	52	69
total carbohydrates (g)	200	300	401
total fat (g)	25	38	50
total saturated fat (g)	3	5	6
total cholesterol (mg)	0	0	0
total sodium (mg)	1078	1617	2156
total fiber (g)	8	12	15
% calories from fat	19	19	19

Colonial Bread

This traditional bread uses ingredients that were commonly found on the colonial farm and has a crunchy texture unique to recipes containing corn meal.

1 lb	1½ lb	2 lb
6 oz warm water	9 oz warm water	1½ C warm water
2½ T molasses	3⅓ T molasses	⅓ C molasses
1½ T butter	2⅓ T butter	3 T butter
2½ T yellow corn meal	3¾ T yellow corn meal	⅓ C yellow corn meal
½ t salt	¾ t salt	1 t salt
1¾ C bread flour	2⅝ C bread flour	3½ C bread flour
¾ t active dry yeast	1¼ t active dry yeast	1½ t active dry yeast

Nutritional Analysis (per loaf, approximate)			
Item	1 lb	1½ lb	2 lb
total calories (kcal)	1240	1847	2504
total protein (g)	32	48	64
total carbohydrates (g)	227	335	460
total fat (g)	22	33	43
total saturated fat (g)	11	18	23
total cholesterol (mg)	46	71	92
total sodium (mg)	1270	1912	2543
total fiber (g)	3	5	7
% calories from fat	16	16	16

Eleanor Roosevelt's Whole Wheat Bread

This recipe was adapted from *The White House Cookbook* (Culinary Arts Institute, Chicago, Illinois, 1968). Mrs. Franklin D. Roosevelt liked wheat bread and served it at many White House gatherings. She enjoyed coarse bread and liked to use fresh stone-ground whole wheat flour.

1 lb	1½ lb	2 lb
2 T molasses	3 T molasses	¼ C molasses
½ T butter	1 T butter	1 T butter
6 oz warm water	1 C warm water	1½ C warm water
½ C whole wheat flour	¾ C whole wheat flour	1 C whole wheat flour
½ T brown sugar	2¼ t brown sugar	1 T brown sugar
½ t salt	¾ t salt	1 t salt
1¾ C bread flour	2⅝ C bread flour	3½ C bread flour
1 t active dry yeast	1½ t active dry yeast	2 t active dry yeast

Nutritional Analysis (per loaf, approximate)

Item	1 lb	1½ lb	2 lb
total calories (kcal)	1257	1911	2514
total protein (g)	39	58	77
total carbohydrates (g)	252	377	503
total fat (g)	11	19	22
total saturated fat (g)	4	8	9
total cholesterol (mg)	15	31	31
total sodium (mg)	1156	1762	2312
total fiber (g)	14	21	28
% calories from fat	8	9	8

Farmer Bread

A traditional white loaf made sweeter by dates and nuts.

1 lb	1½ lb	2 lb
1 egg	1 egg	2 eggs
3 T butter	¼ C butter	⅜ C butter
5 oz milk	8 oz milk	10 oz milk
2 T walnuts, chopped	3 T walnuts, chopped	¼ C walnuts, chopped
2 T dates, chopped	3 T dates, chopped	¼ C dates, chopped
1 t salt	1½ t salt	2 t salt
2 C bread flour	3 C bread flour	4 C bread flour
1½ T sugar	2½ T sugar	3 T sugar
1½ t lemon peel	2¼ t lemon peel	1 T lemon peel
1 t active dry yeast	1½ t active dry yeast	2 t active dry yeast

Nutritional Analysis (per loaf, approximate)

Item	1 lb	1½ lb	2 lb
total calories (kcal)	1603	2343	3205
total protein (g)	46	67	92
total carbohydrates (g)	242	366	484
total fat (g)	50	68	100
total saturated fat (g)	26	36	53
total cholesterol (mg)	292	334	584
total sodium (mg)	2610	3838	5221
total fiber (g)	10	15	19
% calories from fat	28	26	28

Honey Barley Bread

The distinctive flavor of barley is evident in this bread that combines three different types of flour.

1 lb	1½ lb	2 lb
1 C warm water	1½ C warm water	2 C warm water
2½ T honey	¼ C honey	⅓ C honey
2 T wheat gluten	3 T wheat gluten	¼ C wheat gluten
1 ⅛ C bread flour	1¾C bread flour	2⅓ C bread flour
⅓ C barley flour	½ C barley flour	⅔ C barley flour
½ t salt	½ t salt	1 t salt
¾ C whole wheat flour	1¼ C whole wheat flour	1½ C whole wheat flour
1½ t active dry yeast	2 t active dry yeast	1 T active dry yeast

Nutritional Analysis (per loaf, approximate)

Item	1 lb	1½ lb	2 lb
total calories (kcal)	1181	1834	2361
total protein (g)	58	88	115
total carbohydrates (g)	229	358	457
total fat (g)	7	10	13
total saturated fat (g)	1	2	2
total cholesterol (mg)	0	0	0
total sodium (mg)	1128	1159	2256
total fiber (g)	13	22	27
% calories from fat	5	5	5

Mormon Rye Bread

A traditional recipe from the 19th century, modernized to include yeast as leavening.

1 lb	1½ lb	2 lb
3½ oz warm water	5½ oz warm water	7 oz warm water
2 T honey	3 T honey	¼ C honey
4 T shortening	⅜ C shortening	½ C shortening
1 T butter	1½ T butter	2 T butter
½ T sugar	2¼ t sugar	1 T sugar
½ C rye flour	¾ C rye flour	1 C rye flour
1½ C bread flour	2¼ C bread flour	3 C bread flour
2 T brown sugar	3 T brown sugar	¼ C brown sugar
½ t salt	¾ t salt	1 t salt
1½ t active dry yeast	2½ t active dry yeast	1 T active dry yeast

Nutritional Analysis (per loaf, approximate)

Item	1 lb	1½ lb	2 lb
total calories (kcal)	1715	2575	3429
total protein (g)	32	48	64
total carbohydrates (g)	250	375	499
total fat (g)	67	101	134
total saturated fat (g)	21	31	41
total cholesterol (mg)	31	46	61
total sodium (mg)	1202	1804	2404
total fiber (g)	14	22	28
% calories from fat	35	35	35

Mountain Rye Bread

This basic rye recipe will give you the taste of rye with a fluffy consistency.

1 lb	1½ lb	2 lb
1 C water	1½ C water	2 C water
1 T vegetable oil	1½ T vegetable oil	2 T vegetable oil
2 T honey	3 T honey	¼ C honey
1 t salt	1½ t salt	2 t salt
1 T caraway seed	1½ T caraway seed	2 T caraway seed
1 C rye flour	1½ C rye flour	2 C rye flour
1¾ C bread flour	2½ C bread flour	3½ C bread flour
3 T nonfat dry milk	¼ C nonfat dry milk	⅜ C nonfat dry milk
1½ t active dry yeast	2¼ t active dry yeast	1 T active dry yeast

Nutritional Analysis (per loaf, approximate)

Item	1 lb	1½ lb	2 lb
total calories (kcal)	1597	2334	3194
total protein (g)	50	73	100
total carbohydrates	305	445	610
total fat (g)	21	31	42
total saturated fat (g)	3	4	5
total cholesterol (mg)	4	7	9
total sodium (mg)	2272	3407	4544
total fiber (g)	6	9	13
% calories from fat	12	12	12

Mustard Grain Bread

This whole-grain bread features 3 different types of flour and the tang of Dijon mustard.

1 lb	1½ lb	2 lb
½ C warm water	¾ C warm water	1 C warm water
2 T butter	3 T butter	¼ C butter
⅓ C Dijon mustard	½ C Dijon mustard	⅔ C Dijon mustard
1 t sugar	1½ t sugar	2 t sugar
½ t salt	1 t salt	1 t salt
¾ C bread flour	1⅓ C bread flour	1½ C bread flour
½ C rye flour	⅔ C rye flour	¾ C rye flour
½ C whole wheat flour	⅔ C whole wheat flour	1 C whole wheat flour
2 t active dry yeast	3 t active dry yeast	1½ T active dry yeast

Nutritional Analysis (per loaf, approximate)

Item	1 lb	1½ lb	2 lb
total calories (kcal)	1014	1622	2026
total protein (g)	31	50	63
total carbohydrates (g)	161	262	321
total fat (g)	30	46	60
total saturated fat (g)	15	22	30
total cholesterol (mg)	61	92	123
total sodium (mg)	2313	4002	4626
total fiber (g)	11	17	24
% calories from fat	26	25	26

Nutmeg Bread

Try this bread for a spicy treat. Excellent as toast.

1 lb	1½ lb	2 lb
⅔ C water	1 C water	1⅓ C water
1 egg	1 egg	2 eggs
1 T orange juice (frozen concentrate)	1½ T orange juice (frozen concentrate)	2 T orange juice (frozen concentrate)
1⅔ T honey	2½ T honey	3⅓ T honey
1 to 3 dashes salt	¼ t salt	½ t salt
⅓ t nutmeg	½ t nutmeg	¾ t nutmeg
2¼ C whole wheat flour	3⅓ C whole wheat flour	4½ C whole wheat flour
1 t active dry yeast	1½ t active dry yeast	2 t active dry yeast

Nutmeg Bread Nutritional Analysis (per loaf, approximate)

Item	1 lb	1½ lb	2 lb
total calories (kcal)	1129	1694	2283
total protein (g)	45	67	91
total carbohydrates (g)	232	348	469
total fat (g)	11	16	21
total saturated fat (g)	3	4	5
total cholesterol (mg)	213	319	425
total sodium	440	661	1237
total fiber	34	51	69
% calories from fat	8	8	8

Old-Fashioned Herb Bread

This light but spicy bread is great with light meals. It is light textured yet filling and is a suitable luncheon bread, particularly with a soup or salad.

1 lb	1½ lb	2 lb
2 T warm water	3 T warm water	¼ C warm water
4 oz milk	6 oz milk	1 C milk
1½ T shortening	2½ T shortening	3 T shortening
1 egg	1 egg	2 eggs
1½ T sugar	2½ T sugar	3 T sugar
¾ t salt	1¼ t salt	1½ t salt
2 C bread flour	3 C bread flour	4 C bread flour
¼ t ground nutmeg	½ t ground nutmeg	½ t ground nutmeg
1¼ t sage	2 t sage	2½ t sage
1 t active dry yeast	1½ t active dry yeast	2 t active dry yeast

Nutritional Analysis (per loaf, approximate)

Item	1 lb	1½ lb	2 lb
total calories (kcal)	1382	2084	2775
total protein (g)	44	63	88
total carbohydrates (g)	226	342	452
total fat (g)	32	50	65
total saturated fat (g)	9	14	19
total cholesterol (mg)	196	204	394
total sodium (mg)	1717	2815	3442
total fiber (g)	8	12	16
% calories from fat	21	22	21

Old-Fashioned Onion Bread

This bread is ideal with a salad. It can also be dried and used for tasty salad croutons.

1 lb	1½ lb	2 lb
¾ C water	1¼ C water	1½ C water
1½ T olive oil	2 T olive oil	3 T olive oil
2 T molasses	3 T molasses	¼ C molasses
⅔ package* onion soup mix (dried)	1 package onion soup mix (dried)	1⅓ package onion soup mix (dried)
1½ T powdered milk	2 T powdered milk	3 T powdered milk
1⅓ C whole wheat flour	2 C whole wheat flour	2⅔ C whole wheat flour
⅔ C bread flour	1 C bread flour	1⅓ C bread flour
½ t active dry yeast	1 t active dry yeast	1 t active dry yeast

*1 package contains 4 oz of soup mix.

Nutritional Analysis (per loaf, approximate)

Item	1 lb	1½ lb	2 lb
total calories	1302	1916	2623
total protein (g)	40	60	80
total carbohydrates (g)	230	344	463
total fat (g)	30	41	60
total saturated fat (g)	6	8	12
total cholesterol (mg)	13	17	26
total sodium (mg)	2405	3601	5392
total fiber (g)	22	33	44
% calories from fat	20	18	20

Parsley Bread

Try this bread for a variation on the white bread theme. The parsley and garlic add zest to this tasty bread.

1 lb	1½ lb	2 lb
7 oz water	1¼ C water	1¾C water
1 T olive oil	1½ T olive oil	2 T olive oil
4 t parsley, chopped	2 T parsley, chopped	2⅔ T parsley, chopped
½ t minced garlic	1 t minced garlic	1 t minced garlic
1 T sugar	1½ T sugar	2 T sugar
2 T wheat bran	3 T wheat bran	¼ C wheat bran
2 T wheat germ	3 T wheat germ	¼ C wheat germ
2 C bread flour	3 C bread flour	4 C bread flour
1 t active dry yeast	1½ t active dry yeast	2 t active dry yeast

Nutritional Analysis (per loaf, approximate)

Item	1 lb	1½ lb	2 lb
total calories	1244	1866	2487
total protein (g)	39	59	79
total carbohydrates (g)	226	340	453
total fat (g)	20	30	40
total saturated fat	3	4	6
total cholesterol (mg)	0	0	0
total sodium (mg)	24	35	48
total fiber (g)	6	8	11
% calories from fat	15	15	15

Polenta–Millet–Sunflower Seed Bread

When my boys were small, they planted some sunflower seeds in our back yard in Arizona. To their amazement, the plants grew over 10 feet (3 m) tall, and had a large sunflower at the top of each stalk. Sunflower seeds are native to the American Southwest and to Mexico, and have become very popular in American baking. This bread is a wonderful blend of grains with cornmeal, millet, and whole wheat. (*Polenta* is actually an Italian mush that is sometimes made from cornmeal.) There is enough bread flour to give the bread a wonderful, smooth texture that makes it excellent for toasting.

1 lb	1½ lb	2 lb
½ C warm water	¾ C warm water	1 C warm water
2 T honey	3 T honey	¼ C honey
1 T vegetable oil	1½ T vegetable oil	2 T vegetable oil
1 egg	1 egg	2 eggs
¼ t sugar	½ t sugar	½ t sugar
½ t salt	¾ t salt	1 t salt
2 T millet, raw	3 T millet, raw	¼ C millet, raw
2 T cornmeal	3 T cornmeal	¼ C cornmeal
½ C whole wheat flour	¾ C whole wheat flour	1 C whole wheat flour
1¼ C bread flour	2 C bread flour	2½ C bread flour
2 T sunflower seeds	3 T sunflower seeds	¼ C sunflower seeds
1 t active dry yeast	1½ t active dry yeast	2 t active dry yeast

(Nutritional analysis is on next page.)

Polenta–Millet Nutritional Analysis (per loaf, approximate)

Item	1 lb	1½ lb	2 lb
total calories (kcal)	1304	1989	2609
total protein (g)	40	60	81
total carbohydrates (g)	228	355	456
total fat (g)	27	39	55
total saturated fat (g)	4	6	8
total cholesterol (mg)	181	181	361
total sodium (mg)	1135	1675	2269
total fiber (g)	15	23	31
% calories from fat	19	18	19

Potica

This traditional bread is a smoothly textured sweet white bread that is excellent for breakfast.

1 lb	1½ lb	2 lb
3½ T milk	⅓ C milk	⅜ C milk
2 T shortening	3 T shortening	¼ C shortening
2½ T warm water	3¾ T warm water	⅓ C warm water
1 egg	1 egg	2 eggs
2 T butter	3 T butter	¼ C butter
2 T sugar	3 T sugar	¼ C sugar
2 T walnuts, chopped	3 T walnuts, chopped	¼ C walnuts, chopped
½ T grated orange peel	2 t grated orange peel	1 T grated orange peel
1½ t active dry yeast	2 t active dry yeast	1 T active dry yeast

Nutritional Analysis (per loaf, approximate)

Item	1 lb	1½ lb	2 lb
total calories (kcal)	661	957	1312
total protein (g)	11	13	21
total carbohydrates (g)	32	47	62
total fat (g)	57	83	113
total saturated fat (g)	23	34	46
total cholesterol (mg)	249	284	496
total sodium (mg)	316	447	624
total fiber (g)	2	3	4
% calories from fat	75	76	75

Pueblo Sage Bread

Since sage grows wild in the Pueblo country of New Mexico, it is a popular herb among the Native Americans of the area. This bread uses some modern ingredients, but has the age-old flavor unique to Southwestern cooking.

1 lb	1½ lb	2 lb
2 T warm water	3 T warm water	¼ C warm water
1 T cooking oil	1½ T cooking oil	2 T cooking oil
½ C cottage cheese	¾ C cottage cheese	1 C cottage cheese
1 egg	1 egg	2 eggs
1¾ C bread flour	2½ C bread flour	3½ C bread flour
1½ t sugar	2¼ t sugar	1 T sugar
2 t dried sage	1 T dried sage	1⅓ T dried sage
¼ t salt	½ t salt	½ t salt
½ t baking soda	¾ t baking soda	1 t baking soda
1½ t active dry yeast	2¼ t active dry yeast	1 T active dry yeast

Nutritional Analysis (per loaf, approximate)

Item	1 lb	1½ lb	2 lb
total calories (kcal)	1197	1702	2393
total protein (g)	52	73	104
total carbohydrates (g)	188	269	376
total fat (g)	25	34	49
total saturated fat (g)	5	7	10
total cholesterol (mg)	190	195	380
total sodium (mg)	1683	2764	3367
total fiber (g)	8	11	15
% calories from fat	19	18	19

Sesame Honey Bread

Sesame seeds always add a nutty flavor to bread, and this is no exception. It is great toasted with jam or jelly.

1 lb	1½ lb	2 lb
⅔ C warm water	1 C warm water	1⅓ C warm water
2½ T honey	¼ C honey	⅓ C honey
2½ T buttermilk	¼ C buttermilk	⅓ C buttermilk
1 t salt	1½ t salt	2 t salt
2 C bread flour	3 C bread flour	4 C bread flour
2 T wheat bran	3 T wheat bran	¼ C wheat bran
⅓ C sesame seeds	½ C sesame seeds	⅔ C sesame seeds
1½ t active dry yeast	2¼ t active dry yeast	1 T active dry yeast

Nutritional Analysis (per loaf, approximate)

Item	1 lb	1½ lb	2 lb
total calories	1474	2229	2948
total protein (g)	46	69	92
total carbohydrates (g)	262	398	525
total fat (g)	29	44	58
total saturated fat (g)	5	7	9
total cholesterol (mg)	1	2	3
total sodium (mg)	2193	3293	4385
total fiber (g)	4	6	7
% calories from fat	18	17	18

Shaker Daily Loaf

The story goes that a 19th century Kentucky Shaker community member named Sister Virginia originated this bread and baked it daily. Her original recipe yielded roughly 5 lb (2.2 kg) of bread and has, of course, been scaled down for the bread machine. This simple but tasty white bread is an excellent staple white bread, fit for putting on the table while still hot.

1 lb	1½ lb	2 lb
3 oz warm water	4½ oz warm water	6 oz warm water
⅓ C milk	½ C milk	⅔ C milk
1½ T shortening	2¼ T shortening	3 T shortening
1 t sugar	1½ t sugar	2 t sugar
½ t salt	¾ t salt	1 t salt
2 C bread flour	3 C bread flour	4 C bread flour
1 t active dry yeast	1½ t active dry yeast	2 t active dry yeast

Nutritional Analysis (per loaf, approximate)

Item	1 lb	1½ lb	2 lb
total calories (kcal)	1237	1855	2474
total protein (g)	37	56	74
total carbohydrates (g)	208	312	416
total fat (g)	27	40	53
total saturated fat (g)	7	11	14
total cholesterol (mg)	11	17	22
total sodium (mg)	1116	1674	2232
total fiber (g)	8	12	15
% calories from fat	20	20	20

Trail Bread

Rye is a popular grain throughout the world because it will grow in many places where less rugged grains will not. It requires less water than wheat and can grow well in soil of much poorer quality. It was first cultivated in Roman times and quickly became a staple in breads throughout Europe, including Scandinavia and Russia. Since rye is naturally low in gluten content, it doesn't rise much. While the original bread tends to be much denser, for the bread machine we have tried to capture the essence of this bread, although we added more wheat flour to give it a better rise. Substituting rye flour for wheat will work, but take care not to overburden the mixing motor of your bread machine with too dense a loaf.

1 lb	1½ lb	2 lb
½ C warm water	¾ C warm water	1 C warm water
1½ T vegetable oil	2¼ T vegetable oil	3 T vegetable oil
1 T honey	1½ T honey	2 T honey
½ T butter	2 t butter	1 T butter
1 T brown sugar	1½ T brown sugar	2 T brown sugar
½ C whole wheat flour	¾ C whole wheat flour	1 C whole wheat flour
1 C bread flour	1½ C bread flour	2 C bread flour
¼ C rye flour	⅜ C rye flour	½ C rye flour
2 T instant dry milk	3 T instant dry milk	¼ C instant dry milk
¾ t salt	1 t salt	1½ t salt
1 T raisins	1½ T raisins	2 T raisins
1½ t active dry yeast	2¼ t active dry yeast	1 T active dry yeast

(Nutritional analysis is on next page.)

Trail Bread Nutritional Analysis (per loaf, approximate)

Item	1 lb	1½ lb	2 lb
total calories (kcal)	1193	1781	2386
total protein (g)	33	49	65
total carbohydrates (g)	203	304	406
total fat (g)	30	45	61
total saturated fat (g)	7	9	13
total cholesterol (mg)	17	23	34
total sodium (mg)	1722	2307	3444
total fiber (g)	16	25	33
% calories from fat	23	22	23

Texas Bran Bread

This traditional basic bread has a hint of sweetness and a soft bran texture.

1 lb	1½ lb	2 lb
6 oz warm water	9 oz warm water	1½ C warm water
1½ T butter	2 T butter	3 T butter
½ t molasses	¾ t molasses	1 t molasses
1 T brown sugar	1½ T brown sugar	2 T brown sugar
½ t salt	¾ t salt	1 t salt
2 C bread flour	3 C bread flour	4 C bread flour
1½ T bran	2 T bran	3 T bran
1 t active dry yeast	1½ t active dry yeast	2 t active dry yeast

Nutritional Analysis (per loaf, approximate)

Item	1 lb	1½ lb	2 lb
total calories (kcal)	1207	1783	2414
total protein (g)	35	53	71
total carbohydrates (g)	215	322	430
total fat (g)	22	30	44
total saturated fat (g)	11	15	23
total cholesterol (mg)	46	61	92
total sodium (mg)	1257	1856	2514
total fiber (g)	10	15	20
% calories from fat	17	15	17

Nutritional Quick Reference

All the recipes in this book were analyzed for nutritional value. The following lists contain the top 10 breads in each category, in order.

High-Fiber Breads

Haidd: Welsh Barley Bread

Nutmeg Bread

Italian Herb Bread

Herb Bread

Old-Fashioned Onion

Whole Wheat Bread

Peanut Butter Bread

Wheat Corn Bread

Oatmeal Bran Bread

Sweet Potato Wheat Twist

Low-Fat Breads

Prune Bread

English Loaf

Italian Herb Bread

Honey Barley Bread

Honey Mustard Bread

Nutmeg Bread

Quick Onion Bread

Eleanor Roosevelt's Whole Wheat Bread

Feta Garlic Bread

Broa: Portuguese Corn Bread

Low-Calorie Breads

Potica

Broa: Portuguese Corn Bread

Olive, Mint, and Onion Bread

English Loaf

Mustard Grain Bread

Italian Herb Bread

Herb Bread

Light Wheat Bread

Prune Bread

Whole Wheat Bread

Low-Sodium Breads

Parsley Bread

Potica

Nutmeg Bread

Air Bread

Cornmeal Bread

Broa: Portuguese Corn Bread

Festive Hawaiian Bread

Prune Bread

Wild Rice Bread

Buha (Adobe Bread)

U. S. Liquid Measure Equivalencies*
and Metric Conversions

1 cup = 8 fluid ounces

1 cup = 16 tablespoons

1 cup = 48 teaspoons

1 cup = 236 mL

4.2 cups = 1 L

1 fluid ounce = 29.5 mL

1 fluid ounce = 6 teaspoons

1 fluid ounce = 2 tablespoons

1 tablespoon = ½ fluid ounce

1 tablespoon = 3 teaspoons

1 tablespoon = 15 mL

1 teaspoon = ⅙ fluid ounce

1 teaspoon = 5 mL

Abbreviations:

C = cup

T = tablespoon

t = teaspoon

oz = ounce

*These are also used for measuring flour and other dry ingredients in this book.

Bread Machine Information

Use the blanks to enter specific information about your bread machine and then use the chart for handy reference.

Machine Brand: _____

Model Number: _____

Capacity: _____

Basic White Bread Recipe:

Bread Flour _____

Ounces of Liquid _____

Liquidity Ratio _____

About the Author

Norman A. Garrett is a college professor and an expert in computers and technology. He founded his own telecommunications consulting company and has written numerous computer-related books and articles. He received his bachelor's degree from Brigham Young University and his master's and doctoral degrees from Arizona State University. He enjoys cooking and baking, particularly outdoor cooking with old-fashioned dutch ovens.

INDEX